The Radical Christian Life

THE RADICAL CHRISTIAN LIFE
A Year with Saint Benedict

Joan Chittister

LITURGICAL PRESS
Collegeville, Minnesota

www.litpress.org

Cover design by Ann Blattner. *Saint Benedict*, sculpture by Peter Watts, housed at Gethsemane Abbey, Kentucky. Photo by Brother Patrick Hart, ocso. Used with permission.

1	2	3	4	5	6	7	8	9

Library of Congress Cataloging-in-Publication Data

Chittister, Joan.
    The radical Christian life : a year with Saint Benedict / Joan Chittister.
      p. cm.
    ISBN 978-0-8146-3365-6 — ISBN 978-0-8146-3955-9 (e-book)
    1. Benedict, Saint, Abbot of Monte Cassino—Meditations.   2. Devotional calendars—Catholic Church. 3. Christian life—Catholic authors.   I. Title.

BR1720.B45C55   2011
242'.2—dc22   2011016240

CONTENTS

THE RADICAL CHRISTIAN LIFE

An Exercise in Spiritual Imagination

There are two stories, one from the Sufi masters and one from the monastics of the desert, that may have a great deal to tell us about what it means to live a radical Christian life in our own times.

In the first, the Sufi tell about a spiritual elder who asked the disciples to name what was the most important quality in life: wisdom or action? "It's action, of course," the disciples said. "After all, of what use is wisdom that does not show itself in action?" "Ah, yes," the master said, "but of what use is action that proceeds from an unenlightened heart?" Or to put it another way, busyness alone is not enough to qualify us as a spiritual people. We must be busy about the right things.

In the second story from the desert monastics, Abba Poemen says of Abba John that John had prayed to God to take his passions away so that he might become free from care. "And, in fact," Abba John reported to him, "I now find myself in total peace, without an enemy." But Abba Poemen said to him, "Really? Well, in that case, go and beg God to stir up warfare within you again for it is by warfare that the soul makes progress." And after that when warfare came Abba John no longer prayed that it might be taken away. Now he simply prayed: "Lord, give me the strength for the fight."

Point: We are not meant to be long-distance observers of life. We are to give ourselves to the shaping of it, however difficult that may be in this day and age.

This commitment to co-creation is a great task, a noble task for which to give a life, but it is not a simple one. We are at a crossover moment in time—somewhere between the certainty of the past, the demands of the present, and the possibility of the future. It is a moment again in human history that needs deep wisdom and requires holy struggle.

At the dawn of the twenty-first century, the world is shifting. In fact, the world is dizzyingly mobile now. As a culture, we are shifting away from being isolationist and independent to being global and interdependent.

It is a world where "Catholic and Protestant" have melted into simply being Christians together and our new neighbors and their temples, monasteries, and mosques are Hindu, Buddhist, Jewish, and Muslim.

Our task now is to be radical Christian communities—in the here and now—not fossils of a bygone reality, not leftovers from an earlier golden age. Now we need new wisdom and a new kind of struggle to determine what we must be and do in the midst of these changing times.

Our choices are clear: We can go forward again and become something new in order to leaven the new or we can go backward in an attempt to maintain what we know better but which is already gone.

The question is then: What does it mean to be a radical Christian community in times such as these? And how do we do it?

The choice is ours. But, don't be fooled: not only is it not an easy choice; it is not an easy task.

The very map of the world is changing as we stand here: People are starving to death on the television screens in our family rooms. People who have worked hard all their lives fear for their retirement while we continue to put more money into instruments of destruction in this society than we do into programs for human development. The economy is in a state of skew. Only those who do not have to work are really making money. And, at the same time, there are a growing number of very rich and an even greater number of very, very poor.

Life is counted as nothing. Abortion is the most popular form of birth control in developing countries.

Hundreds, thousands, of civilians everywhere—most of them women and children—die in wars that men design to "protect them." And we continue to practice capital punishment even though we know that this so-called "deterrence," which makes us just like what we hate, does not deter. In fact, the ten states without capital punishment have lower murder rates than those that do.

Christians, serious seekers, now must choose either to retire from this fray into some paradise of marshmallow pieties where they can massage away the questions of the time, the injustice of the age, with spiritual nosegays and protests of powerlessness— where they can live like pious moles in the heart of a twisted world and call that travesty peace and "religion"—or they can gather their strength for the struggle it will take to bring this world closer to the reign of God now.

But what can possibly be done in this runaway world of the powerful few by the rest of us who hold no malice and want no wars, who have no influence but hold high ideals, who call ourselves Christian and claim to mean it!

Who are we now? And who do we want to be?

Most of all, where can we possibly go for a model of how to begin to be a radical Christian witness in a society in which we are almost totally remote from its centers of power and totally outside its centers of influence?

My suggestion is that we stop drawing our sense of human effectiveness from the periods of exploration and their destruction of native peoples, or from the period of industrialization and its displacement of people, or from the periods of the world wars and their extermination of peoples.

My suggestion is that little people—people like you and me—begin to look again to the sixth century and to the spiritual imagination and wondrous wisdom that made it new. Because that is really the good news.

An Ancient Model

In the sixth century, Benedict of Nursia was an aspiring young student at the center of the empire with all the glitz and glamour, all the fading glory and dimming power, that implied.

Rome had overspent, overreached, and overlooked the immigrants on the border who were waiting—just waiting—to pour through the system like a sieve.

Rome—ROME!—the invincible, had been sacked. As in the book of Daniel, the handwriting was on the wall, but few, if anyone, read it.

In our own world, the headlines are in our papers, too, and few, if any, are reading them.

But in the sixth century, one person, this young man, resolved to change the system not by confronting it, not by competing with it to be bigger, better, or more successful but by eroding its incredible credibility.

As Blaise Pascal would write: "It is true that force rules the world but opinion looses force."

This one single person in the sixth century—without the money, the technology, the kind of systemic support our age considers so essential to success and therefore uses to explain its failure to make a difference—simply refused to become what such a system modeled and came to have a major influence in our own time.

This one person simply decided to change people's opinions about what life had to be by himself living otherwise, by refusing to accept the moral standards around him, by forming other people into organized communities to do the same: to outlaw slavery where they were; to devote themselves to the sharing of goods as he was; to commit themselves to care for the earth; to teach and model a new perspective on our place in the universe.

And on his account—though numbers, history attests, were never his criteria for success—thousands more did the same age after age after age.

For over 1,500 years, popes and peoples across the centuries have called Benedict of Nursia the patron of Europe and accredited the Benedictine lifestyle that he developed in the darkest periods of Western history with the very preservation of European culture.

The values it modeled maintained the social order. And safeguarded learning. And gave refuge to travelers. And made rules for war that brought peace to chaos.

Those values turned a Europe devastated by invasion and neglect into a garden again. They modeled the equality of peoples. They provided a link between heaven and earth—between this life, chaotic as it was, and the will of God for all of life. Everywhere. Always.

But how was all of that done? And what does it have to do with us today? The answer upends everything our own society insists is essential to effectiveness.

The very model of life that Benedict of Nursia gave the world was exactly the opposite of what, in the end, was really destroying it.

To a world that valued bigness—big villas, big cities, big armies, big systems—Benedict gave a series of small and intense communities where people of one mind gathered to support one another, to find the strength for the fight. Their struggle was for survival, but their strength was community.

To an empire with a global reach—France, Britain, Egypt, Constantinople—Benedict gave an unending line of local groups whose solicitude for the people and understanding of the issues of the area from which they came was built into their very DNA. The struggle of such small groups was for survival, yes; but their strength was total engagement in the human condition.

To an empire intent on the centralization of all cultures into one, Benedict gave a model of autonomy, of agency, of individual self-development to a culture that accepted both submission and slavery far, far too easily. The struggle against such odds was for survival, yes; but their strength was a sense of human dignity and personal possibility—in an era that had neither.

To a world with a bent for monuments meant to mark the history and the glory of an empire, Benedict abandoned the notion of a joint institutional history and built a common tradition out of many separate parts instead. The struggle was for survival of these autonomous small groups. Their strength was the singular commitment bred in each separate group to each carry the fullness of the tradition.

In a civic order strictly defined by specific roles and responsibilities, Benedict chose instead to create a lifestyle rather than to define a fixed work that the years could erode or the culture could abandon. The struggle was surely for survival; but the surety of that in every group was creativity and adaptation.

In a world made up of powerful institutions Benedict did not create an institution; instead, he started a movement—a loose collection of similarly serious and equal seekers who gave the world new ways of thinking about autocracy and narcissism, oppression and injustice, inequality and authoritarianism. The struggle was indeed survival; the strength was an energy and dynamism that affected the whole society.

And finally, in a world where the word of an emperor meant death, Benedict built a world where the word of God gave new life day after day after day to everyone it touched.

A Tradition that Transforms

And little by little, this little movement of serious seekers, small rather than large, local rather than global, autonomous rather than centralized, more intent on a common tradition than a common history, more a movement than an institution, more committed to the Gospel than to the system—bound together as equal adults in communities of heart and mind they crept up slowly on the culture around them, they seduced its hardness of heart, they converted its soul, and, in one small place after another, they made the world whole again.

So why does it work? What can something so small, so fragile, possibly be able to give to a world like that?

How is it that something built on individual members in small individual houses for which survival is always the order of the day can possibly have "saved European culture" and then spread across the whole wide world? After all, individual Benedictine monasteries have come and gone in great number century after century but the tradition has lived on.

The fact is that Benedict left us a very simple structure, yes, but he left it standing on very deep pillars.

He established it on values that spanned the whole human experience—not on rules or specific works that would crash and crumble with the crumbling of the time and cultures.

He based the life on human and spiritual insights that never go out of style: on foundational human needs, for instance, like community and work and service; on profound spiritual practices, like prayer and contemplation and humility; on major social issues, like stewardship and hospitality, equality and peace; on basic organizational givens, like leadership and communal decision making, on mutual service and mutual obedience.

And so as every era grappled with its own agendas and issues, the importance or consciousness of each of these Benedictine values became the gift Benedictines gave to a culture out of sync with its own best interests.

In early Benedictinism, community itself and the need for hospitality, generated by the breakdown of public security that came with the fall of the empire, was the issue. When pilgrims and travelers were being raped, robbed, and pillaged on the roads, these communities built guesthouses—whole hospitality centers—to protect them.

In the Middle Ages, the need for agricultural development and social services became paramount. When whole tracts of land were burned out by war or fell into disuse, when crops died for want of good husbandry, when the peasants were starving and without work, small communities set up granges—small missions of three or four monastics—to organize the laborers and distribute the crops to the poor. And they did these things while they tried, at the same time, to make rules for war that would mitigate its effects and control the seemingly endless insanity that was destroying, ironically, exactly what was being fought for.

With the rise of cities and the dawn of commercialization, the creation of spiritual and educational centers became a major Benedictine concern. Where learning became a thing of the past and whole areas were left spiritually starved, monasteries took upon themselves the preservation of ancient texts and became the spiritual refuge of the poor, the homeless, the oppressed.

In the nineteenth century European Benedictine monasteries sent some of their best to the new world to do the same. It was a world of Catholic versus Protestant cultures, a dying but still potent remnant of the wars of religion long centuries past. The Benedictine task in the new world was to educate Catholic immigrant populations to take their place in a world that was largely WASP—white, Anglo-Saxon, and Protestant. It was a very radical Christian mission for that time to educate the poor and illiterate, integrate sharply divided worldviews into a democratic whole, and adjust to the kind of pluralism the world had never known. And it was successful.

Through it all, for centuries—centuries—Benedictine communities—small, local, and autonomous—worked in creative ways to meet the needs of the areas in which they grew, struggling always to shape and balance a deep and communal spiritual life with the great social needs around them.

They gifted every age out of the treasures of the heart that are the pillars of Benedictinism. As a result, they grew and they concentrated and they specialized and they changed till there were as many slightly different but all basically the same Benedictine monasteries as there were stripes on a zebra.

If the twenty-first century needs anything at all, it may well be a return to the life-giving, radical vision of Benedict. Perhaps we need a new reverence for bold Benedictine wisdom if civilization is to be saved again—and this time the very planet preserved.

The values that saved Western Europe in a social climate akin to our own were creative work, not profit making; holy leisure, not personal escapism; wise stewardship, not exploitation; loving community, not individualism raised to the pathological; humility, not arrogant superiority; and a commitment to peace, not domination. Today, just as 1,500 years ago, those values have been foresworn.

We dearly need them again.

The Pillars of Benedictine Spirituality

Creative Work

This age needs to rethink work. Work in our time has either become something that defines us or something that oppresses us. We do it to make money, money, money or we decry it as an obstacle to life. We are a culture that too often stands between workaholism and pseudo-contemplation.

For years I watched Sophie, an old Polish lady across the street from the monastery, sweep the sidewalk in front of her house with a strong and steady hand and then move methodically to the front of the houses to her left and to her right.

She became, in fact, a kind of neighborhood joke, doing a fruitless task. After all, the street was spotless already, wasn't it? What was the use of this senseless monotony?

And then she died.

Newer, younger neighbors moved into her house who had no time, no interest, in sweeping sidewalks. And the street has never been clean since.

Sophie reminded me again what Benedict's commitment to work was meant to teach us. I recognized in her that the work we do is not nearly so determining as why we do it.

Work—every kind of work: manual, intellectual, spiritual—is meant to be the human being's contribution to the development of the human race.

The Benedictine works to complete the work of God in the up-building of the world. We work, as well, to complete ourselves. We become more skilled, more creative, more effective. When we work we discover that we really are "good for something."

Work, the Benedictine sees, is an asceticism that is not contrived, not symbolic. It's real. It is a task that puts me in solidarity with the poor for whom the rewards of labor are few and far between while the rigors are constant and security is tenuous.

Work is our gift to the future, and if the work we do is a contribution to the order and the coming of the reign of God, and if we do it well, like Sophie, it will be needed, and when we are not there to do it, it will be missed.

Holy Leisure

This age needs to rethink leisure, as well. Play and holy leisure are not the same things. Leisure is the Benedictine gift of regular reflection and continual consciousness of the presence of God. It is the gift of contemplation in a world of action.

Holy leisure is a necessary respite from a wildly moving world that turns incessantly now on technology that grants neither the space nor the time it takes to think.

I remember the day some years ago when a reporter called to ask for an interview on some document that had just been released from Rome.

"I can't talk to you about that," I said. "I haven't seen it and I don't comment on anything I haven't had a chance to read and study."

"Well," he said, "if I send it to you, will you talk to me about it then?"

I calculated the time: This was Thursday. The document couldn't possibly arrive in the mail before Monday, so I figured I could meet the deadline I was working on now and get the new document read before he called.

"All right," I said, "You can send it."

A few minutes later I heard a clacking sound coming from an office down the hall.

"What is that?" I said to the sister in the office.

"It's the fax machine," she said. "It's something for you from New York and it's already over eighty pages long. There's a note on it about calling you back to talk about it this afternoon."

This is a world high on technology, short on time, starved for reflection.

Benedictine leisure is a life lived with a continuing commitment to the development of a culture with a Sabbath mind.

The rabbis teach that the purpose of Sabbath is threefold: First, to make everyone—slave and citizen alike—free for at least one day a week.

Second, to give us time to do what God did: To evaluate our work to see if it is good.

And finally, the rabbis say, the purpose of Sabbath is to reflect on life, to determine whether what we're doing and who we are is what we should be doing and who we want to be. Sabbath is meant to bring wisdom and action together. It provides the space we need to begin again.

If anything has brought the modern world to the brink of destruction it must surely be the loss of holy leisure.

When people sleep in metro stations it is holy leisure that asks why.

When babies die for lack of medical care it is holy leisure that asks why.

When thousands of civilians die from "death by drones"—unmanned aerial predators that bomb their lands and lives unmercifully—it is holy leisure that asks, how that can possibly be of God?

To give people space to read and think and discuss the great issues of the time from the perspective of the Gospel may be one of Benedictinism's greatest gifts to a century in which the chaos of action is drying up humanity's deepest wells of wisdom.

Dom Cuthbert Butler wrote once: "It is not the presence of activity that destroys the contemplative life; it is absence of contemplation."

Holy leisure is the foundation of contemplation and contemplation is the ability to see the world as God sees the world. Indeed, the contemplative life will not be destroyed by activity but by the absence of contemplation.

In Benedictine spirituality, life is not divided into parts, one holy and the other mundane. To the Benedictine mind all of life is holy. All of life's actions bear the scrutiny of all of life's ideals. All of life is to be held with anointed hands.

Who shall lead them into a contemplative life if not we?

Stewardship

The spirituality of stewardship, one of Benedictinism's strongest, greatest gifts, must be rethought in our time.

The 401 pounds of garbage per U.S. citizen that the world cannot dispose of is made up of the Styrofoam cups we use and the tin cans we've discarded rather than recycled while the rest of the world reuses three to five times as much material as we do. Humans today are polluting earth, sea, and sky at a rate unheard of in any other period of history and we in the United States more than most.

But Benedictines before us brought order and organization, learning, Scripture and art, the tools of civilization and the sustenance of the soul.

They used every human form of education and skill to bring order out of chaos, equality to the masses, and healing to their world. Benedictines before us tilled dry land and made it green. They dried the swamps and made them grow. They seeded Europe with crops that fed entire populations, they raised the cattle that gave new life, they distilled liquors and brewed hops that brought joy to the heart and health to the body. It is not possible to live life with a Benedictine heart and fail to nurture the seeds of life for every living creature.

How, as Benedictines, if we are serious seekers, can we possibly build now what is not green? How can we soak our lands in chemicals and grow what is not organic? How can we possibly, as Benedictines, use what is not disposable and never even call a community meeting on the consequences to others of our doing so?

To allow ourselves to become chips in an electronic world, isolates in a cemented universe, women and men out of touch with the life pulse of a living God, indifferent to creation, concerned only with ourselves, and still call ourselves good is to mistake the rituals of religion for the sanctifying dimensions of spirituality.

The serious seeker knows that we are here to become the voices for life in everything everywhere—as have done our ancestors before us for over 1,500 years.

Benedictine spirituality, the spirituality that brought the world back from the edge before, asks us to spend our time well, to contemplate the divine in the human, to treat everything in the world as sacred. We need the wisdom of stewardship now.

Community

Community is a concept that our age must reexamine and renew. An old woman in my Pennsylvania hometown lived alone in her own home till the day she died. The problem is that she died eighteen months before her body was found because no one ever came to visit her, no one called to see if she had gotten her prescriptions, no one checked when her water was turned off for lack of payment. And there are thousands like her in this world of ours.

And how are we reaching out to them? Benedictine community assumes by its very nature that we exist to be miracle workers to one another. It is in human community that we are called to grow. It is in human community that we come to see God in the other. It is in its commitment to build community that Benedictinism must be sign to a world on the verge of isolation.

But a Benedictine spirituality of community calls for more than togetherness—the very cheapest sort of community. Communal spirituality calls for an open mind and an open heart. It centers us on the Jesus who was an assault on every closed mind in Israel.

To those who thought that illness was punishment for sin, Jesus called for openness. To those who considered tax collectors incapable of salvation, Jesus called for openness. To those who believed that the Messiah—to be real—had to be a military figure, Jesus was a call to openness.

The Benedictine heart—the heart that saved Europe—is a place without boundaries, a place where the truth of the oneness of the human community shatters all barriers, opens all doors, refuses all prejudices, welcomes all strangers, and listens to all voices.

Community cannot be taken for granted. We must ask ourselves always who it is who is uncared for and unknown—dying from loneliness, prejudice, or pain—and waiting for your community and mine to knock on the door, to seek them out, to take them in, to hold them up till they can live again.

Real community requires mindfulness of the whole human condition—so that the spirit that is Benedictine may spread like a holy plague throughout the world.

Humility

Humility needs to be rediscovered if we are to take our rightful place in the world in this age. It was July 20, 1969, the night the

United States landed the first man on the moon. I was standing next to a foreign exchange teacher who had come from Mexico to teach Spanish for us.

"Well," I laughed, looking up into the dark night sky, "There's the man in our moon." I could almost hear her bristle beside me. In a tight, terse voice she said back, "It is not your moon!"

At that moment I got a lesson in Benedictine humility, in international relations and racism and multiculturalism that springs from it, that no novice mistress had been able to articulate nearly as well.

Humility is about learning your place in the universe, about not making either yourselves or your nation anybody's god. It is about realizing that we are all equal players in a common project called life.

Learning like that can change your politics. It will certainly change your humanity—your soul.

In a culture that hoards money and titles and power and prestige like gold, Benedict makes the keystone value of his rule of life a chapter on humility that was written for Roman men in a society that valued machoism, power, and independence at least as much as ours.

It is the antidote to an achievement-driven, image-ridden, competitive society that is the hallmark of the modern age.

Humility, the acceptance of our earthiness, is also the antidote to the myth of perfectionism that, masking as holiness, can sink the soul in despair and lead it to abandon the very thought of a truly spiritual life in the face of the very failures we fear.

It makes us look again at our so-called patriotism, our sexism, our racisms, and our narcissism, both personal and national.

It makes us look again even at our spiritual arrogance in the face of the world's other great spiritual traditions.

Most of all, it enables us to learn and to grow and never to be disappointed in what we don't get in life because, we come to realize, it isn't ours to claim in the first place.

We need the wisdom of humility now. We need that quality of life that makes it possible for people to see beyond themselves, to value the other, to touch the world gently, peacefully, and make it better as we go.

Peace

We must, most of all, in our time, rethink the meaning of peace. Over the archway of every medieval monastery were carved the words, *Pax intrantibus*, "Peace to those enter here."

The words were both a hope and a promise. In a culture struggling with social chaos, Benedict sketched out a blueprint for world peace. He laid a foundation for a new way of life, the ripples of which stretched far beyond the first monastery arch to every culture and continent from one generation to another, from that era to this one, from his time and now to ours. To us.

That is our legacy, our mandate, our mission—as alive today as ever, more in need in today's nuclear world than ever before.

Once we could teach that the United States' major export was wheat. Now we have to admit that weapons are. We arm 250 different countries every year and provide almost half of all the arms sold in the world while we decry the selling of them.

Indeed, as Benedictines we must rethink our own commitment to Benedictine peace and our obligation to proclaim it in this world. Benedictine peace, however, is not simply a commitment to the absence of war. It is, as well, the presence of a lifestyle that makes war unacceptable and violence unnecessary.

Even if we dismantled all the war machines of the world tomorrow, it would be no guarantee that we would have peace. The armies of the world simply demonstrate the war that is going on in our souls, the restlessness of the enemy within us, the agitation of the human condition gone awry.

To all these things we need to bring a new spiritual imagination. Imagine a world where people choose their work according to the good it will do for the poorest of the poor—because they saw it in us.

Imagine a world where holy leisure, spiritual reflection rather than political expedience, began to determine everything we do as a nation—because they saw it in us.

Imagine a world where the care of the earth became a living, breathing, determining goal in every family, every company, every life we touch—because they saw it in us.

Imagine a world devoted to becoming a community of strangers that crosses every age level, every race, every tradition, every difference on the globe—because they saw it in us.

Imagine a world where humble listening to the other became more important than controlling them—because people saw it in us.

Imagine a world where what makes for peace becomes the foundation of every personal, corporate, and national decision—because they were called to it by us.

And now imagine what communities inspired by Benedict can do, should do, will do—consciously, corporately, conscientiously—to bring these things into being in every area, region, street, city, institution here and now.

Let us resolve again to follow the fiery-eyed radical Benedict of Nursia whose one life illuminated Western civilization. Let us, in other words, live Benedictine spirituality and illuminate our own darkening but beautiful world.

On the Dialogues of Gregory

A follower of Benedict who became Pope Gregory the Great is attributed with preserving the life of Saint Benedict in a document called The Dialogues of Gregory. The Dialogues are the only source of biographical materials that we have on either Benedict or his sister, Scholastica. Through stories in the metaphorical style of the time, the Dialogues give insight into their personal qualities and character of soul rather than a recitation of simple historical details. The stories are fanciful to modern ears, perhaps, but logical to the heart. These are the things of which real humanity is made: the spiritual life and the human community. As a result, Benedict and Scholastica do not shine in the human constellation of stars because of who or what they are as individuals. No, Benedict and Scholastica stand out in history because of what their lives did for the centuries of lives that would follow them.

It is my belief that the way of life established by Benedict over 1,500 years ago is a gift to our times, a beacon in the dark showing us still how to live well.

THE MENDING OF A TRAY
A Call to Good Work

Benedict was born to a noble family in what is known as Norcia, Italy. As a young man, Benedict was sent to Rome to study. But Benedict, whose heart burned with the love of God, soon became disenchanted with the debauchery of metropolitan Rome. He abandoned his studies and left Rome to pursue his call from God in solitude. He settled in a small village, accompanied only by his nurse.

One day the nurse borrowed a special tray to prepare a meal. But then, inadvertently, she dropped the tray and broke it. The old woman wept. It was a matter to be taken seriously in a place and time where neither mass production nor money were common. Seeing her distress Benedict knelt down, took the two parts of the broken tray into his hands, and, weeping himself, prayed. No sooner had he finished praying than he noticed that the tray was mended and, with great joy, returned it to his nurse.

It is a simple little story, almost laughable to the scientific, rationalist types of our time. Yet it tells us something too long lost, it seems, under layers of data and levels of systems:

It tells us that there is nothing so small that it does not deserve our attention.

It tells us that we must weep with those who weep.

1

It tells us that the lives of the little ones of the world depend on us.

It tells us that every living being has a right to dignity, protection, and help.

It tells us that we must be menders of what is broken in society, not its judges, nor its mocking observers.

January 1

It's World Peace Day. All over the world today—in Haiti, in Palestine, in inner-city Chicago, and in the backwaters of every little town—working people live without dignity. The story of Benedict is a call to take the plight of the poor seriously. The question for our time is: Is it possible to live a truly spiritual life unless we care about the things that the poor care about?

January 2

During the Christmas season we celebrate the Magi who saw the divine where others saw nothing but strangers. And poor ones at that. Learning to see more in life than life itself demonstrates is a gift of true spirituality. Benedict saw in his weeping nurse the broken bits of humanity that have been left behind in the race for money and power in life. Who around you is broken now? And how are you responding as a result of it?

January 3

"What is the deepest meaning of Buddhism, Master?" the disciples asked. And, in reply, the Zen story recounts, the Master made a long, deep bow to his pupil. The learning is an important one: Unless we come to reverence the others in our lives, we will never really give ourselves on their behalf. Worse than that, we will miss much of the beauty of life ourselves.

January 4

"You save your soul by saving someone else's body," Arthur Herzberg wrote. To anyone who would make the spiritual life an escape from reality, an avoidance of human problems, the tale of the broken tray is clear warning that those who ignore a commitment to uphold human dignity everywhere ignore the essence of sanctity.

January 5

Of the billions of dollars spent on world military expenditures, over half of it is spent by the United States. Now. While the poor get poorer everywhere—and even here, as well. Imagine the kind of dignity we could provide for the people in our lives, if we cared enough to protest that waste of money on potential destruction so that it could be spent on human development instead.

January 6

An African proverb reads, "Not to aid one in distress is to kill her in your heart." Clearly what is argued here is the responsibility that each of us has to the dignity of the other. Sinlessness is not enough. Only love is the measure of goodness.

January 7

On this day in 1971, the government banned the use of DDT. It was the beginning of the struggle to save human lives from the effects of toxic chemicals designed, ironically, to enhance natural processes of agriculture. This consciousness of the linkage between life and death, between "progress" and disaster, is a call to spirituality, more now than ever.

January 8

Once upon a time a rabbi asked his pupils how they could tell when the night had ended and the day had begun. "When you know that the animal in the distance is either a sheep or a dog?" the first pupil answered. "No," the rabbi said. "When you can look at a tree in the distance and tell whether it is a fig tree or a peach tree?" the second pupil said. "No," said the rabbi. "Then when is it?" the pupils demanded to know. "Daylight is when you can look into the face of any man or woman and see that it is your brother or sister. If you cannot see that, it is still night." Concern for human dignity is the key to human community.

January 9

In Scripture's story of the baptism of Jesus, the voice of God pronounces Jesus "beloved." Humanity, in other words, is loved by God. All humanity. Yours. Mine. All the other humanity of the world. It is an important concept for us all. How can any of us hope to be "beloved" if we have not loved others enough to give ourselves to bring dignity to another life?

January 10

"Our concern," Rabbi Heschel wrote, "is not how to worship in the catacombs but how to remain human in the skyscrapers." Only those who extend themselves on behalf of those whose lives have lost dignity and are in pain can claim to be truly religious.

January 11

When Benedict's nurse broke the tray she had borrowed, she wept. And so did he. For whose pain do you weep? Correction: have you ever wept for anyone's pain besides your own?

January 12

"To behave with dignity is nothing less than to allow others freely to be themselves," Sol Chaneles writes. Confirm someone's sense of human dignity today by complimenting people you meet on something, however small.

January 13

Samuel Johnson wrote, "The applause of a single human being is of great consequence." The message is clear: What we do to other people can affect their way of being in the world. In other words, the attention and dignity we give to those around us are the seeds of all the relationships in the world.

January 14

Benedict's anonymous nurse is a model of simple people whose future has, for one reason or another, been taken out of their own hands. Benedict took that situation as a responsibility of his own. For whose lives, that do not necessarily touch yours, are you taking responsibility?

January 15

Martin Luther King Jr. was born on this day in 1923. As a small boy he was called "a little nigger" and slapped by a white woman in a public store. He lost his best friend when he was six because he was black and his little companion was white. His father took him out of a shoe store without buying because the clerk refused to fit him unless they moved to the chairs in another part of the store. He knew human indignity and because of that he spent his life concerned about the dignity of others.

January 16

Today's gospel recounts John's recognition of Jesus as special, as marked. "Behold the Lamb of God," he says. Lambs were sacrificial offerings in early Judaism. Jesus gave his life for the human dignity of others. Benedict repeats the parable of caring. In what ways am I retelling the story with my own life?

January 17

Today is the feast of Abbot Antony, an early founder of monastic life. The desert monastics recount that one day God led Antony to the home of a physician in order to show him his equal. "What do you do?" Antony asked the physician. "I heal those who come to me," the doctor said. "More than I need I do not take. More than I can use, I give to the poor and all day long I sing the word *Sanctus* in my heart." Who needs your care today? Have you said *Sanctus* in your heart yet?

January 18

At first reading it seems that there is a chasm of difference between Benedict and the nurse. Benedict is young and she is old; Benedict is concerned about spiritual things and she is devoted to the material needs of life; Benedict is a man and she is a woman. Then the picture clears for us. Here is proof positive that we are called to attend to the other. She took care of Benedict; he took care of her. We all have a piece of creation for which we are responsible. What is yours at the present time?

January 19

Elie Wiesel has written: "When someone suffers and it is not you, they come first." Benedict had a personal agenda that he allowed to be interrupted by an upset old nurse. Whose cry have you permitted to interrupt your life today?

January 20

On this day in 1553 the first lunatic asylum appeared in Europe to control the sick for the sake of the well, at whatever cost to their human dignity. Who is being warehoused in this society and this globe now with whom we should be suffering?

January 21

Vladimir Lenin died on this day in 1924. When the Russian state he envisioned did not materialize, he said, "What was needed to save Russia were ten Saint Francises of Assisi." What was needed to save Russia, in other words, were people who would care tenderly for the dignity, the divinity, of everyone in the system. What poor and broken people are today being denied the kind of care that Francis and Benedict gave? Why?

January 22

The real beauty of the story about Benedict and the mending of the broken tray is not that the tray was mended. It was that Benedict cared enough about little things to spend the spiritual energy it took to mend it.

January 23

"Repent and believe," the Scriptures call to us and the story of Benedict shows us how. First, we must repent of our self-centeredness so that we can see the dignity of others, and second, we must believe that God is with us, working miracles in us for the sake of others. It is a strong and empowering message. We must change our lives to see the needs of others. On what are you concentrating your inner strength? Whose life will be better because of it?

January 24

Today is the feast of St. Francis de Sales, the patron of writers and journalists. He wrote, "Do not look forward to what may happen tomorrow; the same everlasting God who cares for you today will care for you tomorrow and every day. Either God will shield you from suffering or God will give you unfailing strength to bear it. Be at peace then and put aside all anxious thoughts and imaginations." We can have a great deal to do with the way others are able to survive their indignities and sufferings. Name one situation that you have helped to resolve this month. Name one person whose dignity was restored because of you.

January 25

When Benedict prayed over his nurse's broken tray, he knew that it was not just the tray that was broken; it was his nurse's dignity that was at stake, as well. It is yet human beings everywhere who are rejected simply because of their state in life. What Benedict was fixing was his nurse's sense of self. We need to learn to give needy people our full attention, as Benedict did, not simply our donations of old clothes and a couple of pieces of pocket change.

January 26

One hundred million children are deprived of education in today's world and most of them are girls. This is human indignity institutionalized and massive. What are you doing to affirm the dignity of women?

January 27

Benedict took on the suffering of his nurse. He did not try to talk her out of it; he did not minimize it; he did not deny its effect on her self-esteem and dignity in a little village where everyone would have come to know about her failure to care for someone else's property. Most of all, he did not give the situation less than his full attention. What concern for human dignity are you paying lip service to but actually giving very little real attention?

January 28

In 1973, the United States government passed the Endangered Species Act. We have treated so many things with indignity since the rise of industrialism that we run the risk of being destroyed by what we have destroyed. Everything has a value that we have a responsibility to guard. What in your area is endangered now? What are you doing about it?

January 29

"My bread may be a material matter. Another's bread is a spiritual matter," Nikolai Berdyaev wrote. Our own salvation depends on our response to the needs of others. It is not the prayers Benedict prayed that made him holy; it is the prayers he lived out in the pursuit of human dignity that really made him great. Where is the stuff of greatness for you?

January 30

The Scriptures promise, "I will raise up for them a prophet." But prophets are simply people who remind us of the word of God in the circumstances of the present. In a similar vein, an unknown teacher once taught, "If the people will lead—eventually the leaders will follow." Both passages are obvious. The world is waiting for us to stand up and speak the word of God for our time. The human dignity of the entire world depends on it.

January 31

On this day in 1958, the United States launched its first space satellite. Since that time, the world has become one vast window where the poor—whose dignity is battered by the lack of water, the decertification of crop lands, the Western rape of their resources, the exploitation of their labor—watch while the wealthy West turns its back on them and their needs. Etched across the screen, however, is the profile of Benedict weeping over an old nurse and a broken tray. It is time for us to mend and care for, care for and mend, the broken world around us too.

SCHOLASTICA AND BENEDICT

A Call to Conversion of Heart

Benedict had a sister, Scholastica, who also dedicated her life to the pursuit of God. She too founded monasteries and became an abbatial figure. The only story we have of Scholastica is told when Benedict was already an abbot of renown. The incident demonstrates clearly that the brother and sister were emotionally close and, both of them, a spiritual influence on the other till the time of her death.

During one of their annual visits, Scholastica, inspired by the depth of their conversation, asked Benedict to remain overnight in the place where they were meeting in order to continue their talk and reflection on spiritual things. Benedict wouldn't even think of it. It was getting dark; it was time to get back to the monastery; it was time to get on with the regular routine of the spiritual life. Unable to persuade him with words, Scholastica put her head down on the table in deep prayer. Suddenly, out of nowhere, a great storm brought flash floods and Benedict realized that he could not possibly return to the monastery that night. And the Dialogues say, "he complained bitterly." He said, "God forgive you, sister! What have you done?" Scholastica answered simply, "I asked you for a favor and you refused. I asked my God and I got it."

The story is a vein worth mining for a lifetime:

It tells us that law is never greater than love.

It tells us to be intent on pursuing the values of life, not simply its rules.

It tells us that discipline is necessary in the spiritual life but that religious discipline is not enough, that depth is a process and that depth costs.

It tells us that God lurks in strange places. And waits for us. And puts in our paths just what we need in order to become what we are meant to be.

It reminds us that a woman has as much power in the eyes of God as any man and that we must recognize women, too, as spiritual guides.

February 1

It is so easy to get carried away with the importance of what we are doing. Then, everything else in life begins to pale. In this month's story it is clear that Benedict was into developing observant communities. There were rules in that place and the rules were to be kept, even though he saw his sister only once a year, even though there was wisdom to be gained by staying with her. God fractured his rigidity in favor of a greater vision. Has your rigidity been fractured yet? What did you learn from that experience?

February 2

Today is the feast of the Presentation of Jesus in the Temple. Candlemas Day it was called in earlier times when blessed candles were distributed to remind us that the prophets Simeon and

Anna recognized the Christ Child as the Light of the World. It is one of those days when we are called to remember the great vision of life which the church lays before us, not the laws that define its disciplines.

February 3

"The loving are the daring," Bayard Taylor wrote. Love sees a way where there is no way. Scholastica knew that the purpose of law is to bring us to the point where we can go beyond it, where we learn to seek what the law can only point to. Have you ever broken one law in order to keep another one?

February 4

A person can get a lot of personal satisfaction out of keeping rules. It may be precisely when we get most wrapped up in the rules that we may have the most to learn about real spirituality. Scholastica knew that Benedict needed more reflection than he needed rigor at the moment. What do you need now—reflection or rigor?

February 5

Lyndon Johnson said once, "Doing what's right isn't the problem. It's knowing what's right that is the problem." Benedict and Scholastica were torn between religious rigor and religious reflection. He chose for rigor; she chose for reflection. The two goods look even, don't they? But without reflection, rigor can get to be its own god.

February 6

It is a common sight for good leaders to find themselves hounded by the crowds for petty matters to such an extent that the leaders themselves get more wrapped up in activity than in vision. Scholastica insisted on our taking the time to sharpen our inner vision. How long has it been since you just took a book, sat down, read, and then thought about it for awhile?

February 7

Today is the birthday of St. Thomas More, the English martyr and official to the king, who refused to follow laws that his conscience could not sanction. The struggle between Benedict and Scholastica was the struggle between lower and higher laws as well. You see, there are some things more important than important things.

February 8

Have you ever reflected on the laws of the land deeply enough to see if they could possibly square with a conscience formed on love? Segregation, for instance, or capital punishment or abortion or even war? Benedict was concerned with the laws of the institution. Scholastica leaves us with a model of the laws of love. Which do you choose in these situations?

February 9

Francois Mauriac, the great French philosopher, wrote, "No love, no friendship can cross the path of our destiny without leaving some mark on it forever." What friendship, what love has left a mark on you?

February 10

Today is the feast of St. Scholastica, sister of St. Benedict, the woman who was clearly his spiritual equal and one of his spiritual guides. God worked in her for the sake of others. What woman do you know in whom God is working for the good of us all? Do you listen to the spiritual insights of women?

February 11

"What action shall I perform to attain God?" the seeker asked. "If you wish to attain God, there are two things you must know. The first is that all efforts to attain God are of no avail." "And the second?" the seeker asked. "The second is that you must act as if you did not know the first." The lesson is clear: we cannot expect to act out of love unless we have schooled ourselves in the practices that form it.

February 12

Today is the birthday of Abraham Lincoln, president and emancipator. Because of his great-heartedness an entire nation was saved from civil rupture, an entire people was freed from slavery, and we were all given another chance to be worthy of our humanity. Lincoln cared more for the spiritual dimensions of life than he did for its legal precedents. What legal precedents need to be challenged by love today?

February 13

The Scripture tells us that Jesus cleansed a leper, one of the outcasts of society. Most important of all, the Scripture points out, Jesus does it contrary to the law and on the Sabbath. In the doing of it, he becomes ritually unclean himself and becomes what the leper was: one of the marginal of the community. "All reasoning ends in surrender to feeling," Blaise Pascal wrote. Just because a thing is legal, in other words, does not make it either good or right—and in our hearts we know that.

February 14

Today is the feast of St. Valentine, the patron of lovers. Have you ever loved anyone enough to do what you knew was good for them, as Scholastica did, even when they didn't like it, as Benedict didn't? Is there anything you should be doing for someone you love right now?

February 15

William Sloan Coffin Jr. said once, "A spiritual person tries less to be godly than to be deeply human." It isn't easy to allow ourselves to be human once we have set out to be holy. That's why so few of us get to be truly holy. We suppress what we are instead of sanctifying it. What is there in yourself that you fear to face and therefore fail to turn to positive energy?

February 16

Getting to know ourselves and learning to control ourselves are the two great tasks of life. Don't make up strange and exotic "penances" to prove your sanctity to yourself. Simply say no to yourself once a day and you will be on the road to sanctity for the rest of your life.

February 17

Benedict was a disciplined man. He knew the value of establishing a holy routine and following it. He set up his communities around a regime of work, prayer, reflective reading, and adequate rest and nourishment. He expected a bit of each every single day and promised his monastics that if they were faithful to such a routine they would come to the "love of God that casts out fear." Which of those elements of life are you lacking now? Do that one now.

February 18

The thing to remember about Benedict and Scholastica this month is that they were meeting together to "reflect on holy things." They were great spiritual leaders but they had never stopped striving for more spirit or seeking for more wisdom. What do you do to deepen your own spiritual life? With whom do you talk about it? And if you don't, why don't you?

February 19

"All of the significant battles are waged within the self," Sheldon Kopp wrote. It's important to allow for time-out periods in life, as Benedict and Scholastica did, when we allow ourselves to think about the battles we are waging within ourselves at the present time. Why? In the hope that this time we can win something from the struggle that makes us more spiritually adult than we have ever been before.

February 20

The gospels tell of Jesus' journey into the wilderness and the temptations that faced him there. It's an important story because it reminds us that temptations are part of life, part of growing up. We grapple with them often—in some instances for our lifetime—before we come to realize that it is not so much the victory as it is the effort to overcome that is holy-making.

February 21

Life is not about becoming "perfect." The concept of perfection is a trick played on the spiritually unwary to make them think they can arrive at a point beyond which they need not go. No, the spiritual life is about naming our demons so that we can proceed despite them. Benedict's demon may well have been perfection if Scholastica had not freed him from the burden of the impeccable so that he could know the challenge of being flawed. Which of your flaws have taught you the most about life?

February 22

At one point in liturgical history, we covered the statues in our churches during penitential periods to remind us that on our way to heaven we had sometimes lost sight of goodness, had plunged ourselves into the darkness which comes from wandering off a sure path. Benedict knew that staying on the path took discipline; Scholastica knew that the purpose of the path was depth. Which do you need most in life right now: discipline or depth to clear your vision again?

February 23

George Frederick Handel, composer of the great Christian oratorio *The Messiah*, was born on this day in 1685. Handel gave the world both the discipline of musical talent honed to a fine point and the depth of musical talent used to lift the spirit in us all. Everyone has some talent that needs to be disciplined so that others can be enriched by it. Do you see your talent as given to you for the sake of others?

February 24

Gandhi wrote once, "Anything you do may seem terribly insignificant, but it is terribly important that you do it." Too often we dismiss, as Benedict did, the spiritual significance of the unusual act—the visit to the hospital, the conversation with the stranger on the bus, the quotation you write down to pass onto a friend. A life of value is not a series of great things well done; it is a series of small things consciously done.

February 25

Today is the birthday of the French impressionist painter Renoir who was born in 1841. The function of the painter, of course, is to rip the scales from the eyes of the rest of us. Scholastica saw life differently than Benedict did too. Each of them gives us a vision of another dimension of life. She gave us a taste of the possible; he gave us a respect for responsibility. Don't be fooled; they are not opposites. The two are always of a piece.

February 26

"Is there anything I can do to make myself enlightened?" the disciple asked the holy one. "As little as you can do to make the sun rise in the morning," the holy one replied. "Then of what use are the spiritual exercises you prescribe?" said the disciple. "To make sure you are not asleep when the sun begins to rise," answered the holy one. Are you doing spiritual exercises to sharpen the sights of your soul? Start now on one psalm verse a day, one paragraph of Scripture, five minutes of quiet time to center your soul on higher things.

February 27

The gospels tell us that Jesus was transfigured before his disciples and they began to see him as they had never seen him before. In The Dialogues of Gregory, Benedict sees the power of love in Scholastica and is himself transfigured by it. Have you ever been transfigured by anything? How did it change you?

February 28

Noah ben Shea writes, "A miracle is often the willingness to see the common in an uncommon way." Scholastica saw life in a new way when she wanted Benedict to forget the demands of the day for a while. Benedict saw life differently when he saw Scholastica's draw on the power of God. We all need to see the link between the daily and the divine in our lives or else we shall separate the very elements that are necessary to our own full development, a commitment to the commonplace and a sensitivity to the cosmic in which we dwell.

February 29

When you find yourself more likely to cling to schedules, rules, lists, and personal agendas rather than to the needs of those around you, beware. There is something amiss in the compass of your heart.

CAVE AND ROMANUS

A Call to Silence and Sacred Leisure

It was only a matter of time before Benedict's goodness was noticed by many. Goodness is a magnet, the power of which overwhelms even those who believe they are not looking for it. Soon, then, Benedict felt smothered with public attention as the pressure on him increased by the day, distracting him in his attempt to live a calm and centered spiritual life. He knew he had to find a space more suitable for serious reflection and a meaningful life. So he left the village and his nurse and went to live in a cave in Subiaco.

Cave dwelling was not an especially unusual kind of retreat for intensely spiritual persons of the time. It is not surprising then that Romanus, a monk from a nearby monastery, was deeply impressed with the sincerity of Benedict's spiritual search. To mark the legitimacy of that intensity, the old monk clothed Benedict in the style established at the time for religious figures and supported him in his pursuit of the spiritual life. He lowered food down the side of the mountain to him. He guarded Benedict's sanctuary by telling no one of his presence in the area. Most of all, he took care of Benedict at great inconvenience to himself. The food he brought him came from his own plate and he left his monastery to care for Benedict without even asking his abbot for permission to do so.

Without Romanus, Benedict could not have lived the life he did; without Benedict, perhaps, Romanus would never have known the fullness of his own.

The lessons for us and our time from a situation such as this are many:

We all need space and time away from the pressures of our successes.

Silence is an important part of thought.

A talent for solitude is a measure of a person's self-development.

What we nurture in life is what we are and what we give the world.

March 1

The monk Romanus who provided food for Benedict in the cave knew that there were some things in life that deserved to be nourished simply for their own sake. Art is one, music is another, good reading is a third; but the power of the contemplative vision is the greatest of them all. Thanks to the support of Romanus, Benedict became visionary to the centuries. What are you helping to preserve for the next generation?

March 2

The concepts of silence, solitude, and spiritual freedom have immense meaning in a world that is noisy, crowded, and given to a kind of social mania. If there is anything we don't like, it is finding ourselves alone, either physically or intellectually. We too often, perhaps, seek support when what we really need is integrity. When was the last time you found yourself in a very different place than the people around you? And?

March 3

The philosopher Blaise Pascal wrote, "The unhappiness of a person resides in one thing—to be unable to remain peacefully in a room." It is silence and solitude that bring us face-to-face with ourselves and the inner wars we must win if we are ever to live a truly integrated life. Stay in a room alone for an hour and make a list of the things you think about during that time. Which one of those things are you avoiding?

March 4

The first Friday of March is the World Day of Prayer. It is a call to all of us to raise our hearts and minds to something above ourselves, to be aware of a spiritual life in us that is being starved by noise pollution. It is a call to the Cave of the Heart where the vision is clear and the heart is centered on something worthy of it.

March 5

The old monk, Romanus, and the young seeker, Benedict, are together a statement of enormous social relevance in a busy world. First, Benedict teaches us that solitude and silence are necessary to restore the soul. Then, Romanus who supports Benedict in what he is doing rather than prevailing upon him to join his own monastery, shows us that there is no one way to live the spiritual life.

March 6

Jesus' "zeal for God's house," of which the Gospel reminds us, is a quality that is nurtured through silence. In silence we find more to life than life has to offer. Once we achieve that level of spiritual centeredness there is nothing in life that can keep us from transcending the superficial and the transitory.

March 7

When Romanus left his monastery to care for Benedict he never even told his abbot he was going, a very serious fault in early monastic life. Why didn't he tell his abbot? Because taking care of the helpless other supersedes the keeping of any custom. Because no one can either give us or deny us the permission to obey the law above the law in life.

March 8

Today is International Woman's Day. Women are the invisible majority of the earth, most of them isolated from help, too many of them living the silence of the oppressed. The function of silence in the life of the privileged is to be able to hear the voices of the forgotten women of the world and to change things in such a way that being born female is no longer a handicap, that women are no longer oppressed in the name of God.

March 9

Solitude and loneliness are not the same thing. Loneliness is the sign that something is lacking. The purpose of solitude is to bring us home to the center of ourselves with such serenity that we could lose everything and, in the end, lose nothing of the fullness of life at all. When you are alone are you lonely or are you in solitude? If loneliness is what it's about, what you may need most is the cultivation of the richness of solitude.

March 10

Benedict and Romanus both had spiritual freedom. Each of them left the confines of one way of life for the sake of another. We, on the other hand, spend so much time trying to make where we are perfect that we too often miss the opportunity to move outside of it. Are you expanding your own horizons now? If not, what's holding you back?

March 11

"If you want the whole thing, the gods will give it to you. But you must be ready for it," folk wisdom teaches. There is absolutely nothing in life that is not destructive if done in excess. Freedom of spirit is the ability to see all the dimensions of life, as Romanus and Benedict did, and to move from one to another without being enslaved by any of them.

March 12

Silence is an intriguing concept. It is only silence that enables us to hear. But silence is a very noisy thing. When we finally start to listen to our own garbled selves as well as to others, we discover how full of static our hearts and minds really are. Silence, the time of coming to inner quiet, is the only chance we have of coming to real peace with life as it is for us. It took Benedict three years in that cave. And you?

March 13

Meister Eckhart wrote, "There is nothing so much like God in all the universe as silence." And the Scriptures remind us that "God so loved the world" that Jesus became the Word of God among us. Alive. In our midst. Like us. Rather than come in power, God came silently in Jesus so that we could discover divinity at our own pace.

March 14

Sri Ramakrishna said, "Do not seek illumination unless you seek it as a man whose hair is on fire seeks a pond." The spiritual life is not gained by osmosis. It must be attended to; it must be sought. Passionately. Benedict knew that there was no hope for his spiritual development if he gave himself over to miracles. Interesting, isn't it? Even good things can become too much of a good thing.

March 15

St. Cyprian taught, "It's a barren prayer that does not go hand in hand with alms." Romanus, holy man that he must have been, is a clear sign for us of someone who realized that there was something more required of him in life than routine, even the best of routines. The only reason for any of us to live the disciplines we do is to become something bigger than what we are.

March 16

If Western culture resists anything at all, it is silence. We pump sound into every available space—on elevators, on boats, in bedrooms, on city streets. Better to do than to think, I suppose, because if we ever really thought about the world we've created, we might change it. And think of all the people who would lose money on that one.

March 17

"If you are afraid of loneliness," Chekhov wrote, "don't marry." Is it possible that the breakdown of so many marriages might really be the result, not of selfishness, but of the propensity to demand from another what we have not been able to develop in ourselves?

March 18

"My loneliness was like a letter I carried with me, and glanced at nervously, and folded and unfolded, but never read," Sy Safransky wrote. Silence calls us to go down into the hollow of ourselves

and wrestle with our loneliness, asking day after day, What growth
is it that God is calling me to right now that will fill my life with
more than myself?

March 19

The feast of St. Joseph, the silent one, who knew in his heart
that to abandon Mary for something, simply because he did
not understand it, was wrong. That's what silence is all about.
It teaches us that the cacophony around us is only a shadow of
the struggle inside.

March 20

Everyone has to be willing to allow one form of themselves
to die so that what they are really meant to be can come to life.
Or, as Lewis Carroll put it, "There is no use going back to yes-
terday for I was a different person then." It is the willingness to
develop into something new, to see new dimensions of life, that
is freedom of spirit.

March 21

The Solemnity of St. Benedict. Learning to live with ourselves,
finding that enriching enough and profound enough, is prelimi-
nary to living with anyone else well. Solitude is an antidote to
dependence.

March 22

The first book ever printed, the Gutenberg Bible, was published on this day in 1457. Until that time books were made by hand, manuscripts were rare, ideas spread slowly. Imagine. No books, no radios, no TV's, no crowds. Just silence. Be consciously silent for one hour today and see what you hear. What does it say to you?

March 23

It doesn't take much living to realize that performance punishes. Whatever we do well, we will be called on to do to the limit. Like Benedict, everybody has to have a cave—a place and a time to take care of themselves before their talents devour them. What's your cave? When were you in it last? For how long?

March 24

Abba Sisoes, one of the early Desert Monastics, taught, "Seek God and not where God lives." Once we have made up our minds that something is good for us it can be so difficult to trust that God may be somewhere else for us as well. That's when we resist change. That's when we cling to the tried and true. That's when we begin to substitute the seeking for the sought, religion for God, the way for the end. That's when we need the freedom of spirit that enabled Romanus to stretch his horizons far enough to find God working another way in his life.

March 25

Today is the feast of the Annunciation, the moment when doing the will of God brought Mary into total solitude, outside the understanding of her society, beyond the support of her family. It is the practice of solitude that enables us to stand alone in life against the ruthless tide. Simone Weil wrote, "Absolute attention is prayer." Have you known the solitude that brings absolute attention to the thought of God? Then you have known the Annunciation.

March 26

When Benedict met the monk Romanus, he met wisdom on the way and put himself under the older monk's care. Who knows whether or not Benedict would have been able to persist in his silent and single-minded search for the presence of God if it had not been for Romanus. Who is the wisdom-figure in your own spiritual journey? Give thanks for that person today.

March 27

Jesus found himself alone in a crowd that chanted his name but ignored his teachings. It was a political messiah the crowd was looking for, not the messiah of the Beatitudes. No wonder Jesus went into Jerusalem sad. Rejection is the worst kind of solitude. It plunges us where we would not be, into the empty depths of life. Clearly, the important thing is to make a friend of solitude so that no amount of isolation can break the crystal of the spirit.

March 28

On this day in 1979 at Three Mile Island, the United States came desperately close to the country's first nuclear power plant disaster. Then, the silence was finally broken on the inherent danger of technology that cannot be contained, controlled, or disposed of safely. Then, we learned the real value of contemplation: it is to see the world as God sees the world and to announce it.

March 29

When Benedict went into the cave at Subiaco, he did not go there to escape the world. He went there in order to get the world into proper perspective. There is so little silence in our world—in our cities, in our families, in us—that we never get the chance to assess anything. We just keep accumulating static, drowning one thing out with another until we have no perspective at all. Practice silence. It is a prescription for mental health in a chaotic world.

March 30

A day without the balm of silence, the wholeness of solitude, is an inhuman day. Helen Keller wrote, "Everything has its wonders, even darkness and silence, and I learn, whatever state I may be in, therein to be content." And, Helen Keller, born both deaf and blind, would surely know.

March 31

A Hindustani proverb teaches, "The true nobility is in being superior to your previous self." Benedict's passage through the hermitage at Subiaco is our model for that. Each of us grows through stages in life, sloughing off one after another of them, like a butterfly its cocoon. The purpose is to come out of each more beautiful than when we went into it. That is the purpose, the price, and the power of the cleansing times of solitude, the reflective times of silence.

POISONING OF WINE
A Call to Purity of Heart

Though he lived alone in a cave as a young man, Benedict's reputation for holiness spread throughout the countryside. The monks from a nearby monastery prevailed upon Benedict, despite much reluctance on his part and only after much persuasion, to become the abbot of a monastery that was failing and leaderless. Clearly, the group had lost its way and had deteriorated. Benedict, the monks realized, had the vision and spirit it would take to save the place. So they convinced him to leave his cave at Subiaco and go with them. It was a potentially great enterprise, this preservation of a monastery, and clearly worth his efforts, his interest, and the redesign of his own life's agenda. He went.

When the community realized, however, what it would demand from each of them to really revive the place, to take it to the heights of its own ideals, they balked. And, to stop the difficult and hated process, they set out to kill this respected and effective abbot by poisoning his table wine. When Benedict took the cup to give it his customary blessing, the vessel broke and he realized immediately what had happened. "You didn't have to do this," he said to the community. "You could just have asked me to leave."

And then Benedict responded in a way that is key to the story: he left that place and went back to live alone with himself.

The implications of the story are far too clear:

Not to confront evil—as Benedict did—is its own kind of evil.

It is not possible to save a thing from itself.

Those who achieve success can become a target for those who are not themselves capable of it.

The important thing in life is to have a center so sound that nothing outside ourselves can disturb it.

April 1

It is so easy to want the good in life but not be willing to make the changes it will take to achieve it. We want to lose weight but we don't eat less. We want to get a promotion but we don't want to work longer hours. We want to live a more balanced life but we don't want to stop anything we're doing now. The fact is that we really want other things more. The question is, What do I really want far more than I want to lose weight?

April 2

Jealousy is the other person's problem. My problem is to build an inner life so rich that it cannot be destroyed when those who want what I have finally get it.

April 3

The sign of complete serenity in life is to be able to lose all the externals and not notice. Silesius wrote, "One has not lived in vain / who learns to be unruffled by loss, by gain / by joy, by pain."

April 4

The difference between us and Benedict is that our self-esteem is tied up in our need to succeed. Benedict simply did what he could as well as he was able, and when that was not accepted, he simply went back to being what he had always been. Christopher Morley wrote, "Success is the ability to spend your life in your way and not to give others absurd, maddening claims upon it."

April 5

"All cruelty springs from weakness," the Roman Seneca wrote. It is so easy just to get in line in life: to never question war; to never speak up for the persecuted; to never "get involved." Most disturbing of all, is that we learn to call that kind of great cruelty "patriotism," and "faith," and "minding our own business." What is the real cruelty from which that kind of denial springs?

April 6

Change is one of the constants of life. It is also one of the most difficult elements of life. We say we want to do it but we want to do it painlessly. We elect people to lead us through change and then we destroy them when they do. The ability to accept change, then, becomes the measure of our willingness to grow. It is always a mark of our maturity.

April 7

"The policy of being too cautious is the greatest risk of all," Jawaharlal Nehru taught. We like risk best when the outcome is guaranteed. What Benedict models for us by leaving his cave and taking on a monastery that he is later forced to leave is the willingness to change the very direction of our lives in the face of another good. The question, you see, is not, Did we succeed? The question is, Did we try?

April 8

There is nothing we can lose in life that does not teach us something worth knowing. Sometimes we learn to pick our friends more carefully; sometimes we learn not to be so committed to what the world calls "success." Sometimes we learn that we have been about the wrong things entirely in life. But there is no such thing as failure as long as we learn something from it. Or, as Michele de Montaigne wrote, "There are some defeats more triumphant than victories."

April 9

"I would rather fail in a cause which I know must someday triumph than succeed in a cause that I know must fail," Wendell Wilkie taught. We must never sacrifice principle to short-term approval. It is a life lesson hard-won on the institutional ladders, at cocktail parties, and in the coffee klatches of the world, but it may be the only lesson worth learning at all. Benedict didn't coax, cajole, and compromise with a recalcitrant group on the grounds that change was slow and patience was more important than truth. He unmasked the evil and left that place. Have you ever disclaimed a group because of its basic dishonesty? What happened to you as a result?

April 10

When Benedict left the monastery that resented his efforts to renew them enough to want to kill him for it, he did nothing whatsoever to justify himself either to them or to the public. He simply went back to being who he was before he ever met them. It is a very liberating model. After all, it is what we are when there is nothing else in life to distinguish us that is the real gauge of a person's quality.

April 11

When the monks set out to poison Benedict because he was expecting more of them than they intended to give, the heart loses a beat. Sadness sets in. Benedict was destined to defeat, not because he wasn't right to expect more of the monks, but because they themselves weren't willing to do more than what had brought them to this pathetic point. The best of saints, the finest of leaders, can't make us be what we have made up our mind not to be. How sad. Is there anything you could have been that you refused to be because you didn't want to make the effort? How do you feel about that now?

April 12

It is so easy to hate what exposes us for what we are. We are not the vocalist we would like to be so we hate the person who can really sing. We are not the star we wanted to be so we hate the stars around us, and work against them, and try to bring them down. Jealousy corrodes the soul. Look carefully at what you hate without cause. It may be telling you a great deal about yourself.

April 13

"Non-cooperation with evil is as much a duty as is cooperation with good," Gandhi wrote. The question is, of course, Why was there not one single monk who resisted the plot against Benedict? And then there is a question even worse than that, What evil is there that I myself have never resisted? Never sent a postcard about it to a politician; never said a word at a cocktail party; never raised a single question in a church group on an obvious evil. No wonder the world is in the situation it is.

April 14

The graffiti in a Filipino prison at the height of the Marcos regime read, "Those who would give light must endure burning." It says nothing at all about having the light accepted. It's only when we define success as achievement that rejection is any kind of problem at all.

April 15

"Those who respect themselves are safe from others; they wear a coat of mail that none can pierce," Longfellow wrote. The message is clear: to be safe from the destruction of others, we must care enough for ourselves not to fear the evaluation of anyone else. What is important is that we develop ideals and then measure up to our own standards. Name two standards that you have set for yourself in life. Have you met them? What would it take?

April 16

"No more duty can be urged upon those who are entering the great theater of life than simple loyalty to their best convictions," Chaplin said. Name a time when you abandoned your own convictions. What did you gain from it? What did you lose?

April 17

"A fox dressed up in sheep's clothing," the rabbis say, "is still a fox." There are some people, some situations, that are simply not worth wrenching our own lives to convert. The die is cast. Their minds are made up. They don't want to change, they can't change, and they won't change here, now, for you. But that's all right. "Shake the dirt from your feet," Jesus says. Give your energies where they'll do the most good. Are you wasting your life on something like that right now?

April 18

"When the pupil is ready the teacher will appear," the Zen teachers say. Nothing ever changes in our lives until we are ready to change it. What is bothering you right now that only you can stop from continuing? What is it inside you that keeps you from doing that?

April 19

A Malayan proverb teaches, "Don't assume that simply because the water is calm that there are no crocodiles in it." It's when we put our trust in a situation itself—government, money, connections, titles—for our sense of well-being and achievement that we jeopardize both our happiness and our future. Do well whatever you need to do at the time, but do not give your entire life to anything that is impermanent—and everything is.

April 20

When Benedict blessed the cup of poisoned wine, it broke. A miracle? Perhaps, but no more a miracle than what we perform when we insulate ourselves from the ignoble around us by nurturing only the good in our lives. Name something gracious in your own life right now. Think of it six separate times today. You will find out that those thoughts break the hold of sadness in your life and drive out the bad. A miracle?

April 21

Benedict agreed to do what he did not want to do because it seemed to be a noble and necessary act. Who knows why the enterprise really failed. Maybe what he lacked at the beginning of the exercise he achieved through it at the end: self-knowledge and self-acceptance. The project, after all, may have been as much for his enlightenment as for the monks. What have you learned about yourself the hard way?

April 22

Jealousy is a kind of insanity. It distorts the way we look at all of life and leaves us agitated and unwhole inside. The only cure for jealousy, ironically, is a holy love of self.

April 23

It may be exactly what we do not like in life that is most necessary for our own development. What we are resisting most may be exactly what we need. What is it for you?

April 24

An Arab proverb teaches, "I must set my face to the wind and scatter my handful of seeds. It is no big thing to scatter seeds, but I must have the courage to keep on facing the wind." Where in life are you facing the most opposition? Don't flinch. Who knows when the wind will change?

April 25

Benedict's experience teaches us one thing clearly: we must never regard failure as failure. It may simply be what is needed to turn us in the direction we should have been going in the first place. Name one of your successful failures.

April 26

Violence is the unchained demon in ourselves, not the evil in the other. Benedict had become "enemy" to the monks he'd come to lead so they set out to poison him. "You didn't have to do this," Benedict said when he realized the plot. "All you had to do was to ask me to leave." All they had to do, in other words, was to be honest with him. They didn't have to sink to their own lowest depths. Is there something unsaid in you that is coming out in worse ways?

April 27

"The only thing necessary for the triumph of evil is for the good to do nothing," Edmund Burke wrote. But if that's the case, then all the evil in the world belongs to us. Now what do you think about that?

April 28

When Benedict left the monastery without a struggle to go back to what he'd been doing before, he gave us all a lesson in the fine art of letting go, whatever the circumstances. The point is not to leave a place in either vengeance or vindication. The point is to have enough inside yourself to carry you despite whatever people have taken away.

April 29

"Everything can be taken from us but one thing," the psychiatrist Victor Frankl wrote, "the last of the human freedoms; to choose one's attitude in any given set of circumstance." It is an important insight when we're under pressure.

April 30

Some wag wrote once, "The pessimist feels things could not be worse. The optimist finds consolation in the fact that they certainly could." There's wisdom in the saying. Don't give up.

PLACID AND MAURUS AND THE MOVEMENT OF MONASTERY

A Call to Community

The holiness of the hermit Benedict spread and he attracted many followers. As a result he was able to found twelve monasteries in the area. Noblemen began to entrust their sons to him, among them the young boys Placid and Maurus.

Three of the flourishing monasteries were at the top of a mountain, far from the waters below. It was a wonderful place for a monastic retreat but it was hard living for the monastics there. They had to walk the mountains every day of the year— under the blistering sun and in the dangerous rain, despite the biting wind and through the hot, thick undergrowth carrying pails of water for cooking and cleaning and personal needs. As far as the monastics were concerned, they explained to Abbot Benedict, it was time to move the monasteries.

Benedict listened but under no condition did he want to move. This was the right place to be. This was the right way to live. There was nothing to be gained by starting over, by moving down the mountain closer to the river and away from where they could concentrate on what they were doing in peace. What's worse, there was a great deal to lose if they did. Clearly, something had to be done to bring both visions together.

That night Benedict went to the top of the mountain with the boy Placid, prayed over a spot, marked it with three stones and the next day directed the monastics to dig there for water. "If you dig down a little, you will see that almighty God has the power to bring forth water even from that rocky summit and in his goodness relieve you of the hardship of such a hard climb," Benedict told them. The monks began to dig and, almost immediately, an abundant spring of water flowed.

It's an important story for all of us who are struggling to make our lives and our relationships fit. It helps us to remember the basics:

Love listens.

People can be totally committed to one another and still have unique individual needs.

Relationships have to be worked at from both sides.

Things can lose their luster and still be right for us.

May 1

The problem with love is that we expect it to last without tending to it. We do better than that with radishes.

May 2

Sometimes our great goals in life—the good work, the promotion, the house in the suburbs—get in the way of our relationships in life. That's when things really get hard. The trick is not to choose one or the other. The trick is to make both of them possible.

May 3

"The true opposite of love is not hate, but indifference," Joseph Fletcher wrote. It would have been so easy for Benedict simply not to care whether the monastics liked the situation as it was or not. He could simply have said, "This is monastic life, take it or leave it." "This is what my work demands, take it or leave it." "This is what I want, take it or leave it." "This is what I'm going to do, take it or leave it." But he didn't. Love listens. Love negotiates. Love satisfies.

May 4

When things are very hard we should try to change them, of course. Too often, however, the temptation is to try to escape them instead. Then, we abandon the good we already have instead of simply learning to doubt our own certainties in the first place so that good can be preserved and good can be achieved at the same time.

May 5

We give ourselves in small ways for great goals and then discover that the giving is not achieving the goal at all. That's what Benedict learned from the monastics. Carrying small pails of water up and down a rugged mountain was not enhancing their monastic life at all. Don't correct people when they tell you that something isn't working with comments like, "Well, that's marriage." Or, "I told you I was going to do this." Or, "You never said anything about not liking it before." Or, "You knew it was going to be like this." Instead, change something. Maybe even in yourself.

May 6

"When a blind person carries a lame person," the Swedish proverb teaches, "both go forward." We all have different needs. A relationship does not dissolve the needs of one of us in favor of the needs of the other. What it should be doing is making it possible to meet the needs of both.

May 7

Sue Frankel-Streit said, "There are times in the lives of all people of conscience when the truth in one's heart is in such deep opposition to the falsehood of the world that one must put everything else in life aside and act upon the truth." Learning to do that takes practice, though. Courage is something we learn, not something we're born with. It's through doing little things that we become capable of doing greater ones. The story shows us how that works: when the monastics took their problem to Benedict, they were taking a great risk themselves. What if he simply said no? On the other hand, how else could he have the chance to say yes? The honesty of their need changed him, too. What truth in your heart have you failed to speak because you feared the response of the one who needed to hear? Practice telling your truth. You'll be surprised what it does both for your personal life and for the life of the world around you.

May 8

A Sufi proverb teaches, "When the power of love overcomes the love of power, there will be true peace." Benedict clearly loved the monastics in his monasteries more than he loved his authority. In fact, he went to great lengths himself to make life better for them. What husband, what wife, what lover can say the same?

May 9

Perhaps one of the reasons for the breakdown of marriage, the cooling of friendships, the loss of love lies solely in the fact that too many relationships revolve around the needs of only one of the people involved. What's worse, it becomes so taken for granted that no one even notices that it has happened. The only sign of it—until it explodes in midair—is a tiny, niggling disease. Are your relationships intact? What have you done for the other persons in your life lately, not because it's a treat, but because it's a need? And how often do you do it?

May 10

When Benedict went out to pray for water he took Placid, one of the younger monastics, with him. It was his way of teaching the future generation the cost and shape of love. "What is the best thing I can do for my children?" the young husband asked his spiritual director. "Love their mother," the holy one answered back.

May 11

It is so easy to do great things for the world around us. It is so human to do sustaining things for those whom we claim to love. Which are you, great or human? Better yet, have you learned to be both?

May 12

No one can satisfy anyone else's needs completely. All we can do is try. Then we have to allow the people we love to find their own way so that they can take their life into their own hands, take responsibility for it, take its consequences on themselves. Benedict didn't dig the well for the monastics. He simply acknowledged the need for it, prepared the way for it, and enabled them to find it for themselves. Parents would do well to proceed the same with children, perhaps; friends with one another; spouses with each other. No one exists for our satisfaction. They only exist to help us find our own.

May 13

"I am not impressed by religion that finds God in God and ignores that image elsewhere," Maria Sylvano writes. Maybe not, but ignoring the image of God in the people around us is more common than we like to think. It always happens, for instance, whenever anyone or any institution decides that they are God's will for someone else.

May 14

Think of the agitation, the frustration, the downright irritation that happened in you the last time someone questioned your procedures or wanted to amend your well-thought-out plans. You know, the ones you planned for their own good—the family vacation, the weekend activities, the work schedule. Now ask yourself again: What was it that you really loved when you made those plans?

May 15

What we owe one another is not direction, it is kindness.

May 16

To be able to face the difficulties of our lives, to admit them and resolve them instead of trying to swallow them in a cauldron of muffled anger, may be the greatest gift we can give those we say we love. It certainly beats resenting them for the rest of our lives and punishing them secretly for doing what we never told them not to do.

May 17

Like Placid, watch carefully when the people around you attempt to mend their mistakes with one another. You have the opportunity to learn how it's done—or at least how it shouldn't be done. If they don't do it by changing their own behavior, suspect it.

May 18

Benedict clearly made one mistake: he never asked the people he was committed to caring for in life whether he was caring for them in the way they needed to be cared for, so he missed their needs completely. Have you ever asked that question yourself?

May 19

Dag Hammarskjold wrote, "Life only demands from you the strength you possess. Only one feat is possible—not to have run away." It's always easier to fantasize ourselves out of a difficult situation than it is to reshape it. Yet, unless we face the difficulty, we may never discover what we were supposed to learn from it.

May 20

Faced with two alternatives, choose always the third. The monastics saw only two possibilities—to carry the water or abandon the site. Those are the kinds of conclusions that too often destroy more than they resolve. Don't get caught in the allusion of alternatives. You're smarter than that.

May 21

Faced with the destruction of his life's work, his life's dream, Benedict held on for the extra minute it took to trust God and try again. Is there anything in your life that you gave up on too soon? Is there anything now that you are tempted to abandon without giving it a chance to change? Why?

May 22

The classic confrontation is "us against them." The classic love story is "us for one another."

May 23

The community could have revolted against Benedict. Others had, remember? Instead, this good group simply opened up the question that led their leadership to new vision, new effort, new results in their behalf. It's amazing what cooperation can do.

May 24

Don't ever be afraid of a question. Don't ever be afraid to try new things. Don't ever be afraid of one another. It is such a waste of time.

May 25

Love at its best is love that respects the distress of the other and does not get in its way, does not try to suppress it or deny it or ignore it. Real love works it out.

May 26

The worst thing you can do is to try to talk people out of their emotions or to tell them that their experience isn't valid. That's why so many conversations fail. I try to tell you something and you try to tell me that I don't really mean it. Oh, yeah?

May 27

"It is better," George Whitefield wrote, "to wear out than to rust out." Maybe those monastics would have been better off just to go on carrying the water up and down the mountain. I don't know. What do you think?

May 28

I understand why those monastics wanted to change monasteries. Wouldn't it be great if you could just quit one thing in life and know for sure that you would never regret it?

May 29

When you have a goal yourself, it is so hard to believe that someone else's goal, obviously in opposition to yours, can possibly be reasonable, valid, understandable. "Be kind," John Watson wrote. "Everyone you meet is fighting a hard battle." That's the kind of thing the monastic Benedict is really teaching us in this story.

May 30

There is one holy goal in life: to refuse to make life more difficult for others than it already is. Then, if I can truly do that, the difficulties of my own life can only disappear.

May 31

Adaptability may be the one great saving quality in any group, in any leader, in any person. The group that is adaptable will last through time. The leader, parent, thinker who is adaptable will be able to negotiate every crisis, every challenge. The person who is adaptable will never be destroyed by any one incident in life. If you ever have to choose between authoritarianism and adaptability, and you want to survive it, choose adaptability.

STORY 6

June

NEAR DROWNING OF PLACID

A Call to Friendship

One day Benedict sent the young disciple Placid to fetch water. Impatient, maybe, or just inexperienced, Placid let the bucket fill too rapidly, lost his balance, and was pulled into the lake, where the current quickly seized him and carried him from shore. When Benedict realized what had happened, he ordered another young monk, Maurus, to go to Placid's rescue. But first, Maurus begged Benedict for a blessing. Then Maurus rushed down the mountain, ran straight across the surface of the water to where Placid was flailing for his life, and dragged him back to safety, amazed himself at what he had done.

The story is an important one for friends and disciples alike. It gives us layers and layers of life to think about:

Like Maurus, it is unlikely that most of us would have done anything of real significance in our lives if we had not been called to it by someone else.

Everyone needs a wisdom figure in life who gives direction, confidence, and spiritual guidance.

Friendship calls us beyond ourselves to love without expecting return, to live without counting costs. Friendship is our ability to see the needs of the other.

57

The miracles in our lives are seldom of our own making. They are simply the function of a few loving friends, the people around us who care enough to call us beyond our own definitions of ourselves.

Love inspires.

June 1

What we find in the people we love is what we are looking for in ourselves. When the disciple Maurus asks Benedict for a blessing he is really asking him for that portion of his spirit which Maurus knows is lacking in himself. To whom do you look for direction in life? What does that tell you about what you need to develop in your own life?

June 2

It is not easy to direct other people. What if they really can't do what we think they should do and therefore trying it destroys their self-esteem? What if they don't want to do it and it erodes their willingness to try other things? Then what? Benedict gives us the key. Our task in the life of the other is simply to point out what is needed; to give the gift of confidence to them and then to wait with patience to see what miracles they work. Force, control, and manipulation are not the fabric of either spiritual direction or of friendship.

June 3

The Irish say, "It is in the shelter of each other that the people live." Placid got into trouble by his own making. He got out of it because one generation was watching out for him and another generation was willing to immerse itself in it with him. We all need both guides and partners. The lonely times in life are when we try to do without either.

June 4

Maurus did what he did for two reasons: first, because he had been called to it by someone wiser than himself and, second, because it was worth doing. A call and a purpose are the axles on which life turns. Who has called you to life? In what are you involved that is life-giving to someone else?

June 5

Benedict sent Maurus to the aid of Placid. He did not tell him what to do there. It was Maurus who ran across the water to the boy. It was Maurus who did more than he ever thought he could humanly do. Think of a time when you did something far beyond what you would have thought you were able. Looking back, how do you explain it?

June 6

Kahlil Gibran said, "Friendship is always a sweet responsibility, never an opportunity." It is so easy, so natural, to look at the others in our lives as tickets to our own comfort. We expect them to do things for us when actually, it is what we do for them that is the measure of the love. Friendship is our pledge to share the life of the other without expecting reward for ourselves. What is your definition of friendship?

June 7

Perhaps the most interesting part of the Benedict story is that Placid went for the water alone, Benedict saw the accident when he was alone, and Maurus was sent to the rescue alone. And yet, each of them needed one another in order to discover something new in themselves—abandonment, insight, and courage. It is a vivid and vital demonstration of real love. Friendship that controls, smothers, and demands is not friendship at all. It ties us down and eats us up. It saps what it should be supporting. Do your friendships create you or consume you?

June 8

For too long we have put the responsibility for human relationships and values on women who were mothers. Each of us, woman and man alike, married or unmarried, has the responsibility for mothering—soothing, caring for, raising up, giving life to others. The day this idea becomes the coin of the realm, war will cease, abuse and battering will cease, destruction will cease. When we are not mothering, we are not being friend to the world.

June 9

Every great spiritual tradition is filled with prayers for good harvest. Every tradition, even in today's technological world, depends on other cultures to sustain it. And yet today much of the world is still starving for something—for food, for peace, for love. Today make a special effort to bring to someone else whatever it is that they most need now.

June 10

It is so tempting to want people to brave their way through trouble and not bother us with their problems. After all, they got into the situation by themselves; they should get out of it by themselves, right? But when Placid was going under, Benedict sent help. Who has rescued you in life? Whom have you ever rescued?

June 11

Phyllis Bottome said, "There are two ways of meeting difficulties: you alter the difficulties or you alter yourself meeting them." What we cannot change around us demands a change inside of us. What are you facing now that you cannot change? What change is it demanding inside of you?

June 12

In going first to Benedict for a blessing before racing into the water, Maurus teaches us that we each need the support of someone wiser than ourselves before we throw ourselves into situations for which we are not prepared but cannot avoid. Then good direction helps us tap into the reservoir of our hearts. Goethe wrote, "You cannot teach a person anything; you can only help them find it within themselves."

June 13

George Bernard Shaw wrote, "No one who is occupied in doing a very difficult thing, and doing it very well, ever loses self-respect." If you do not feel good about yourself, maybe it is because you are not working at something beyond what you think are your capabilities. Find something more challenging to do and life will blossom for you.

June 14

Love costs. It does not always feel good. It sometimes depresses. It always challenges. But it never hurts; it never attacks; it never abandons. Love is what led Maurus to throw himself against a stream too strong for him, a river too wide for him, a water bed too deep for him. Love is the only thing that makes family doable after romance has faded, the chemistry has calmed, and excitement has gone its way.

June 15

"Friends cherish each other's hopes. They are kind to each other's dreams," wrote Thoreau. Too many times we insist on loving people the way we want to love them instead of the way they need to be loved. What we cannot give them, we do not want them to get from anyone else and fear that, if they do, they will love us less as a result. What a pathetic definition of friendship.

June 16

Joseph Addison taught, "Great souls by instinct / to each other turn / demand alliance / and in friendship burn." Sometimes it happens: you simply meet someone who brings another piece of life to your soul like a missing corner of a jigsaw puzzle. That is not acquaintanceship. That is grace, something designed to provide presence when you consider yourself most alone, something meant to call us to grow in depth, self-understanding, and the healing balm of self-revelation.

June 17

Though it was Maurus who ran across the water to him, Placid knew that he had really been rescued by Benedict. It was Benedict's influence in both their lives that made both of them more than they would have been without him. But friendship is like that. The function of friendship is to give us confidence in ourselves, make us free to do what we need to do for others.

June 18

A visitor once said of the eighteenth-century Hasidic rabbi Dov Baer, "I didn't travel to Mezritch to hear him teach, but to watch him tie his shoelaces." It is not what our friend does for us that matters. It is what the friend demonstrates of beauty and goodness that is the essence of holy friendship.

June 19

The Arabic proverb teaches, "Get close to the seller of perfumes if you want to be fragrant." The friendships we develop determine the quality of our own souls. What kind of friends do you choose?

June 20

"Sometimes our light goes out, but it is blown again into flame by an encounter with another human being. Each of us owes the deepest thanks to those who have rekindled this light," wrote Albert Schweitzer. When our energies ebb, when our own hope dies, it is the energy and hope of the other that holds us up and coaxes us on. Name someone who has rekindled a light in your own life.

June 21

Beware of false friends, the ones who want you for their own emotional comfort, the ones who never sense the difficulties of your situation, the ones who want to control you, not leave you free. What masks as friendship is so often simply emotional dependence with a chain. Remember Goethe's warning, "We are shaped and fashioned by what we love."

June 22

"Friendship is a single soul, dwelling in two bodies," Aristotle taught. That's why Benedict could "see" Placid's predicament. That's why Maurus could go to him without thinking of his own safety. That's why Placid could trust the support of his friend without pulling them both down.

June 23

Robert Southey said, "No distance of place or lapse of time can lessen the friendship of those who are thoroughly persuaded of each other's worth." When souls really touch, it is forever. Then space and time disappear and all that remains is the consciousness that we are not alone in life.

June 24

The Egyptian proverb teaches, "An onion with a friend is a roast lamb." Sometimes nothing matters but presence, not time, not conditions, not circumstances. When that is the case, friendship has broken out. Treat it tenderly and consciously and well.

June 25

Benedict clearly loved the young Placid but he did not pretend to be able to do everything the boy needed. When Placid needed another kind of gift to save his life, Benedict realized it, stepped aside, and sent Maurus. Yet, in the end, Placid knew that it was really the love of Benedict that had saved him, much as he owed his life to the love of Maurus as well. Would you allow your friend to have another friend equally loved, equally important to them? Or would that threaten your own sense of well-being, in which case, do you need friendship or self-esteem?

June 26

Auden said, "Among those whom I like or admire, I can find no common denominator; among those I love, I can: all of them make me laugh." Beware of friendships that are too tragic, too filled with personal angst. Friends are people who make life better, not worse; joyful, not stressful; life-giving, not tense.

June 27

The story of Benedict and Placid is a consoling one. Friendship is a quality of life that knows no boundaries. Friends who are older than we are, bring wisdom and calm to our lives. Friends who are younger, bring energy and possibility. Have you ever had a friend who was far older or younger than you? What did it bring out of you? What did it save in you?

June 28

"I never knew how to worship until I knew how to love," Henry Ward Beecher wrote. Friendships that are real, friendships that engage the soul, are glimpses into the eternal love of God. When we really love someone else with a love that is total and a love that is true, then we know how God loves us. It is a breathtakingly unbearable discovery, isn't it?

June 29

Sir Edward Bulwer-Lytton knew what was missing in the world a long time before the woman's movement made us look at the emotional deprivations that sexism creates. He taught, "It is a wonderful advantage to a man . . . to secure an advisor in a sensible woman. In woman there is at once a subtle delicacy of tact, and a plain soundness of judgment, which are rarely combined to an equal degree in man. She will seldom counsel you to do a shabby thing, for a woman always desires to be proud of you." Women-friends are good for both women and men. Do you have at least one?

June 30

Tennyson wrote, "Tis better to have loved and lost / Than never to have loved at all." Sometimes, it's true, we lose something we have loved. And who knows why? What is really important in the end is that, having lost a love, I never lose either the measure of its quality or the depth of its learning. That is the immortal dimension of every friendship, its bridge between us and the rest of the world, the everlasting mark of it on what we call ourselves, the tinder of what it has inspired in us forever.

FOUNDING OF MONTE CASSINO

A Call to Prophesy

This is a story about Benedict and change.

Harassed constantly by enemies who resented his growing popularity and the changes he wrought, Benedict moved constantly on, developing new monasteries, extending his vision, speaking his truth. At the summit of Monte Cassino, Italy, the area that would eventually become his largest monastery and the center of his order, he discovered a flourishing temple to the Roman god of war, Apollo.

He spared no time, brooked no cautions, temporized with nothing, and coaxed no one. He simply did what had to be done and let his world readjust to the stark new reality. He destroyed the statues; overturned the altars; cut down the trees in the sacred groves; dedicated the site to Martin of Tours, the Christian soldier-pacifist who refused to kill; and, where the statue of the god of war itself once stood, he built a chapel in honor of John the Baptist.

After a period of time, the people of the countryside were won over by his zealous preaching. There was apparently no politicking here, no patient persuasion, no pleading, no begging for support and understanding. Just this: Where a vision long dead, well stale, and clearly limiting had been, he brought new voice, new life, new direction.

The challenges to our own lives are clear and unsettling ones:

There are some things in life so serious that they must be confronted directly.

The idols of life must be overturned.

Change is hard and change is slow but there can be no change at all until people are confronted with a new vision.

Change does not come in life by hoping for it. It comes when we do it.

July 1

Dorothy Day and Benedict of Nursia would have understood one another very, very well. Day wrote, "As you come to know the seriousness of our situation—the war, the racism, the poverty in the world—you come to realize that it is not going to be changed just by words or demonstrations. It's a question of risking your life. It's a question of living your life in drastically different ways." And you? Do you understand them? Or are you still hoping to change the world by making no waves?

July 2

Idols are easy to identify when they're made of statuary. It's the ones in our hearts that are more difficult to recognize. Name three things you cling to—clothes, money, position, control, a person—because your life would have to change substantially if you ever had to give them up. Those are your idols.

July 3

Name two organizations to which you belong. Does either of them do anything to effect social change? Change, not charity. What have you learned from that?

July 4

"Living," said Marcus Aurelius, "calls for the art of the wrestler, not the dancer. Staying on your feet is all; there is no need for pretty steps." When the earth shakes under our feet, it is enough just to simply stand there so all the world sees that kind of resolve and takes hope.

July 5

The idols of the age—militarism, sexism, racism, the rape of the earth, abortion on demand—are bringing us to our knees as a culture, wasting our money, halving our human resources, blinding our vision. And still they persist. Why? Because as Helen Keller taught us, "Science may have found a cure for most evils; but it has found no remedy for the worst of them all—the apathy of human beings."

July 6

In July of 1945, the United States made the decision to drop the first atomic bomb on Hiroshima, the devastating power of which we could only calculate theoretically. It was an experiment. On civilians. For the stated purpose of saving soldiers. That day we made militarism our god and since that moment the human needs of civilians around the globe have been sacrificed on the altar of nuclearism. Who will tear this temple down?

July 7

Pindar wrote, "Forge thy tongue on an anvil of truth and what flies up, though it be but a spark, will have light." Have you ever spoken out against an idol of the time? Not complained, not simply agreed with the people who were working against it, but really spoken out yourself, really given it light? What did you learn from that situation?

July 8

"Gradually," Gregory says in the Dialogues, "gradually, the people of the area were won over" after Benedict destroyed the temple of Apollo. It takes time for people to accept a new vision, but they never will until someone supplants the old one with the new and then stays to explain why the change had to occur.

July 9

"Change that is unwilled," the holy one said, "is change that is real." What change was forced on you in life which, eventually, you came to see was far better than you could possibly have imagined? Did it change your attitude toward changes? Why or why not?

July 10

Benedict could have waited and allowed the temple to stand until the people came to see its emptiness themselves, but he didn't. He tore it down. What changes in life would you like to see right now that you have yet to say or do anything about publicly? What stops you? Maybe that is the idol you worship more than you revere the sanctity of the change.

July 11

The idols that we worship are the measure of ourselves. The smaller the idol, the smaller the self. What do you worship? What is its real size in life?

July 12

"The ultimate measure of a person is not where they stand at times of comfort and convenience, but where they stand at times of challenge and controversy," Martin Luther King Jr. taught. Beware of those who say they want social change but insist that they want to get it by making no waves, tipping no boats. They want security a great deal more than they want justice. Most of all, perhaps, they want to look very, very good in public.

July 13

"A solid rock is not disturbed by the wind; even so, a wise person is not agitated by praise or blame," the Dhammapada records. When there is conviction within us, we do not play to the audience, we do not say only what people want to hear, and we do not crumble in the face of opposition. We go on, not because we expect to succeed, but because we cannot live with ourselves unless we do.

July 14

Every society builds its idols. What are the idols of your nation? How does each of them affect your personal life? Why do you keep them?

July 15

An idol is anything that pretends to be what it is not, that seems to satisfy when it can't, that becomes the protected center of our lives. It is the sacred cow to which we sacrifice everything else.

July 16

Jacob Riis wrote, "When nothing seems to help, I go look at a stonecutter hammering away at a rock perhaps a hundred times without as much as a crack showing in it. Yet at the hundred and first blow it will split in two, and I know it was not that blow that did it but all that had gone before." Cracking idols takes the hundred and first blow. What idol are you working on now? Don't quit.

July 17

Benedict must have taken a great deal of public criticism, public rejection, public scorn for overturning the statue of Apollo. After all, the glory of Rome was in its armies if nothing else. He stood up to the most revered of national idols, in other words, and called it false. And "eventually" they listened. It takes courage to stand up to a thing; it also takes courage to wait for others to understand.

July 18

Bishop Desmond Tutu taught, "If you are neutral in situations of injustice, you have chosen the side of the oppressor. If an elephant has his foot on the tail of a mouse and you say that you are neutral, the mouse will not appreciate your neutrality." It's not important to have all the resources necessary to resist evil. It is only necessary to resist. It's a question of morality.

July 19

Benedict didn't simply tear old idols down: Benedict put something new in their place. It is not sufficient to criticize a system. It is imperative that we begin to model ways to live within it differently.

July 20

"Those who reject change are the architects of decay," Harold Wilson wrote. Pagan Rome fell but Christian Rome rose in its place thanks to those who, like Benedict, saw its idols and toppled them. Who will they say toppled the idols in the United States today? You, I hope.

July 21

The Sufi say, "Every morning I cast my seed to the wind. It takes no courage to scatter seeds but it takes great courage to go on facing the wind." Change comes very slowly. Stay with it.

July 22

"Time changes nothing," the proverb teaches. "People do." This means, of course, that all the things that should be different will stay just the way they are until we do something about them. What are the chances of that?

July 23

One of the hardest things in life may be to raise a question, suggest an alternative, begin a new process where none has been sought. But unless we do, who will?

July 24

Everybody wants change. Few are willing to pay its price. Not a single movement in history has succeeded without people smashing idols and people being upset by it. Not one. Sad, but true. Tragic, but necessary. Slow, but imperative. Smash an idol today: ask one unacceptable question.

July 25

Women all over the world are taking axes to the idols of the patriarchy—in homes, in offices, in churches, in government. Someday people will realize why and, like the villagers of Monte Cassino, begin to understand what Christianity really looks like as a result.

July 26

Don't think for a minute that you will get through life without having to make a choice between idols and ideals.

July 27

Patriarchy, militarism, and racism; money, power, and fame; beauty, clothes, and social status are all types of idols that sour our souls and shrivel our hearts to the important things of life. Have you ever been captive to an idol? How did you break it?

July 28

It's one thing to take Quixote-like swings at popular idols; it's another thing entirely to do it alone as Benedict did. That's courage; that's virtue; that's of God. Pray for the grace of that kind of insane hope.

July 29

The point is that Benedict could simply have built a chapel to John the Baptist someplace else. He didn't have to choose Monte Cassino where a temple already stood and a congregation clearly functioned. But he did. He did not merely avoid the issue. He confronted it. And you?

July 30

Name one thing you stand for strongly enough to stand for it alone in the crowd.

July 31

"Courage is resistance of fear, the master of fear, not the absence of it," Mark Twain wrote. Do not be afraid to be afraid. If we wait for our fears to go away, we will never do anything in life but whine in trepidation. What a pitiful way to live a noble life.

TOTILA THE GOTH
A Call to Humility

Totila was king of the Goths, one of the Germanic tribes that breached the borders of the Roman Empire when Rome was no longer strong enough militarily to maintain its boundaries against foreign immigrants. This is clear: Totila was a ruthless marauder. He was also a curious creature. He had heard about Benedict—the simple monk, yes, but also a prophet, leader, and spiritual strongman of the time. The thought of making contact with him firsthand was too fascinating an experience to miss. The very idea of it was too much fun for Totila to even think of passing up. So, he made an appointment to see Abbot Benedict himself. To test Benedict's gift of prophecy, or to tease his troops, maybe, he sent his servant Riggio to the meeting disguised as himself. He could hear the stories over beer and beef already: "And there was Riggio, my horse guard, dressed like me! Ha! ha! And the great holy man bowed and scraped. Ha, ha! Some prophet, ha, ha! He never even knew the difference!" Except that he did.

When Riggio, dressed in fine garments and attended by servants, approached him, Benedict looked at him quietly and said, "Son, take off those gowns. They do not belong to you." The laughing stopped. The meeting ended. Riggio was embarrassed. Totila was sobered to the core. We ourselves are left with a lot to think about:

People see through us when we pretend to be what we are not.

Wearing a mask does not make us what or who we are pretending to be.

Being free to be ourselves is one of the great achievements of life.

All the things in the world can't make us something we aren't.

August 1

One of Eleanor Roosevelt's personal assistants, Mary McLeod Bethune, was black. On one of Eleanor's frequent public trips in the '40s, the two of them were seated together in a first-class railroad compartment working on national projects when the conductor informed Miss Bethune that blacks were not permitted in first-class cars. She would have to move, he said, to one of the back cars. Eleanor Roosevelt was shocked at the situation and immediately began to protest the move. "That's all right, Mrs. Roosevelt," Mary Bethune calmed her. "I don't mind going to a second-class car in the least because, when I get there, it's gonna be first class." Now that's what you call authenticity. Can you name two places where you were told you didn't belong? How did you feel about it? Why?

August 2

"What we anticipate seldom occurs," Disraeli wrote. "What we least expected usually happens." Totila and Riggio learned that the hard way. I know that I did too. What's the best way to prepare for that? Maybe there is none. Maybe it is simply an exercise in faith.

August 3

Ellen Glasglow writes, "All change is not growth; all movement is not forward." Name a change you have been part of that did not reflect spiritual growth and social progress. Call that the Totila syndrome. Now name one that did. Call that the Riggio effect. What was the difference between the two?

August 4

Riggio was pretending to be something he was not. Most of us do the same at one time or other. What are you pretending to be right now that you are not? Why are you doing it? Where's it going to lead if you keep it up?

August 5

Benedict saw right through Riggio and saved Riggio from the empty life that is a pretender's fate. If you're lucky, someplace along the line someone has seen through you too and told you so. Who was it? What changed in you as a result?

August 6

"We lie loudest when we lie to ourselves," Eric Hoffer wrote. Ask Totila. He didn't fool Benedict but he fooled himself to the level of the pitiable. He really thought he could outwit quality by derision and get away with it. Be careful what you set out to deride. You may simply be exposing yourself.

August 7

You have to feel sorry for Totila. Whatever his delusions of grandeur, the people rejected him entirely. As Quentin Crisp said, "The very purpose of existence is to reconcile the glowing opinion we have of ourselves with the appalling things that other people think about us." That's called reality. Have you been faced with it yet? Did you survive? How?

August 8

What we think about ourselves affects everything we do in life: how well we do in school, the friends we choose, our goals in life. To succeed in life we have to be confident enough to learn, sure enough of our own value not to need to be anyone else, proud enough to be our best, and secure enough in our own gifts to be accepting of everyone else's. Now there's a fitness program to be envied.

August 9

There are two life lessons that take some people the greater part of a lifetime to learn: the first demands that I discover who I am—what I, myself, really want in life and what I need to give in life if I am ever to be whole—and the second lies in giving myself permission to be myself no matter who tries to persuade me to be otherwise. Have you managed to learn either one of those lessons completely yet?

August 10

Pretense freezes the soul. One of the most consistent of spiritual lessons from the ancient world—taught by spiritual guides long before psychology as a discipline even existed—is that in order to make progress as a human being we must each be thoroughly known by somebody. Self-exposure is key to growth. Is there anyone in the world with whom you are completely open? Completely?

August 11

Dressing up in someone else's clothes didn't disguise Riggio. To go from horseman to king takes more than clothing. If you live with someone in disguise, you know what I mean.

August 12

Have you ever been around anyone whose every word is affected or every move is exaggerated or every response is canned? Pathetic, isn't it? Wouldn't you love to know who's hiding under there and what they're really thinking? Why don't you ask them someday?

August 13

When strong women have to pretend to be female females, and gays are forced to pretend that they aren't, and very average men are taught to brag so that no one can see how really average they are, and minorities are forced to suppress their own cultures in order to fit into the establishment, that's the kind of pretense that sears the soul. Then people die before they ever begin to live.

August 14

"We had better appear what we are, than affect to appear what we are not," Francois de la Rochefoucauld wrote. Translation: Better to be yourself than to play someone else—poorly.

August 15

Maya Angelou says, "My mother said that I must always be intolerant of ignorance but understanding of illiteracy. That some people, unable to go to school, were more educated and more intelligent than college professors." Name three people you know who are the real thing whether the world has recognized that or not.

August 16

What is there about yourself that you would not want anyone to know? Isn't that funny? We're all hiding the same thing.

August 17

"I am as my Creator made me," Minnie Smith wrote, "and since the Creator is satisfied, so am I." Think of all the musicians who want to be linguists, and all the welders who want to be woodworkers, and all the teachers who want to be writers. Poor souls. Imagine spending your whole life looking into a mirror, unsatisfied. Not only would that take a lot of time, but it would also waste a lot of energy that could be used to make the world better.

August 18

"The human heart, at whatever age," Marie Edgeworth writes, "opens only to the heart that opens in return." Go on, try it.

August 19

Oscar Wilde wrote, "We live in an age when unnecessary things are our only necessities." We drape ourselves in clothes and jewelry and cars and adult toys. And we stay just the way we are inside. It isn't what we have on the outside that defines us. It is what we have inside that determines our real quality.

August 20

Totila, the king, forces Riggio to put on a disguise and pretend before Benedict to be the king himself. It didn't work. Who are you pretending to be? And for whose sake? As Alexander Pope put it, "I am His Majesty's dog at Kew. Pray tell me, sir, whose dog are you?" Is it worth it?

August 21

The story tells us that Benedict told Riggio to take off his dishonest robes; it doesn't say that Benedict showed less respect to Riggio when he was in peasant clothes or more respect to Totila when he was dressed in kingly robes. Are you as attentive to the garbage collector as you are to the local clergy? If not, aren't you precisely the reason that people dress up to fool us?

August 22

"Just remember, we're all in this alone," Lily Tomlin teaches. What we can't have inside ourselves we can't count on to save us. All the robes and trappings in the world did not make Riggio Totila. And, come to think about it, why Riggio would have ever wanted to be Totila in the first place is impossible to understand. Did you ever want to be somebody that now you're glad you aren't? Why did you change your mind? What does that say to you?

August 23

Don't be afraid to be yourself. Jesus wasn't.

August 24

Take a moment to be grateful for all the times and people who enabled you to put down the masks that hid you from the world or from yourself. Thanks to them, you have a chance to become what you really are.

August 25

Here's the thing about Totila: he wasn't simply a skeptic; he was disrespectful. It is one thing to take the private measure of a person. It is another thing entirely to humiliate a person, publicly, as Totila intended to do to Benedict. That's not just bad taste; that's very bad judgment. After all, who trusts you after that?

August 26

"Cautious, careful people, always casting about to preserve their reputations . . . can never effect a reform," Susan B. Anthony taught us. What reputation are you protecting right now? If you weren't worried about your reputation, what would you change about your life?

August 27

When Totila refuses to go himself to see Benedict, he admits that he wouldn't recognize quality if he saw it. That's the problem with arrogance. It makes the arrogant look bad.

August 28

It is not what we are that counts. It is what we are meant to become that matters.

August 29

"This above all: to thine own self be true / And it must follow, as the night the day / Thou canst not then be false to anyone." I memorized that quotation from Shakespeare at an early stage in life but only understood its real meaning stages and stages later. It cost me when I didn't understand it—and it cost me when I did. Which price would you rather pay?

August 30

When you're choosing friends, remember the German proverb, "When the fox preaches, look to your geese." People who do not have the courage to be themselves, do not have the character to be trusted. After all, like chameleons, they will change their personalities to suit the situation. Better an honest struggle than slick little social tricks any day.

August 31

Learning to become ourselves—our best selves—is the very purpose of being alive.

AGAPITUS AND VIALS OF OIL

A Call to Stewardship

This is a story about Benedict and risk and holy anger and the poor. In this story the world intrudes on the monastery with awful directness. It is a time of crop failures, famine, and social breakdown. The poor, caught on arid land, are keenly affected. With no goods to barter, no harvest to sell, no staples to sustain them, honest and hardworking people are reduced to begging. It is a painful time, even for those of social station.

One of them, the subdeacon Agapitus, in a state of desperation apparently, turns to Benedict's monastery for help. And Benedict, overcome with pity, orders the monastery's business manager or cellarer to give him the very last vial of the monastery's oil, a staple and necessity of the day. But the cellarer, an efficient and sensible man, aware of the impact that action could have on the monastery itself, did not do it. When Benedict, a charismatic visionary, realized what had happened, he became very angry. He called the cellarer to his room, took the vial of oil out of his hands, and, in the sight of the entire monastic community, ordered another monk to throw the vial out the monastery window. Then, point made, Benedict had the unbroken vial brought back and given to Agapitus. Benedict rebuked the cellarer in front of the community, knelt down, and began to pray. Suddenly, an empty oil-cask in the room began to fill with oil, overflowed the rim, and covered the floor.

It is a stark and shocking scene and it says a great deal to our times:

It says there are values beyond security and good sense.

It says anger is an instrument of God.

It says everything we have belongs to the poor.

It says the challenge of leadership is to lead us to live beyond ourselves.

It says that those who give to others will be filled themselves with whatever things they need.

September 1

"The greatest enemy of any one of our truths may be the rest of our truths," William James wrote. The cellarer of the monastery valued good stewardship so much he forgot to value the spirit of the Gospel even more. The lesson is an eternal one: Life's major problem does not lie in choosing good from evil. That's obvious and easy. No, life's real problem comes in choosing good from good. What's the answer? That's also easy: when values are in conflict, always choose the higher one.

September 2

Agapitus went to the monastery for help because he had been told that the people there were more devoted to the Gospel. What he found there, however, were people far more devoted to themselves than to the thought of laying down their lives for anyone. The shock of the circumstances saddens us, yes; but in reality the situation may be more common than we like to admit, clergy or no clergy. Saying one thing but living another can get to be an art. What does your organization claim on paper to be committed to doing? Name three things you did this year that would prove it to the public.

September 3

"The next message you need is always right where you are," Ram Dass said, and when Benedict responded to Agapitus, he clearly agreed with the idea that God calls us through human events. What life message are you getting right now from your immediate circumstances or from the people who live with you? How do you feel about it? What is happening in you as a result?

September 4

Lily Tomlin once said, "Once poor, always wantin' rich is just a way of wantin' bigger." Agapitus and the cellarer were both poor. The problem is that only Agapitus knew it. When we know our poverties, we can ask for help. Otherwise, we are inclined to think that we can be self-sufficient. Then, we take care of ourselves first.

September 5

The need for security can be such a block in life. It keeps us where we are, yes, but, worse, it can keep us from discovering where we must be if we are ever to grow to full stature. Benedict shattered security for his monks and made them real monks in the doing. What is security doing for you at this time in your life?

September 6

We cringe at the thought of Benedict's anger. He threw the vial of oil right out the window. Are saints supposed to do those things? Well, as Templeton said, "If we had been holier people, we would have been angrier oftener." What is going on in the world that you should be developing some anger about if the world is ever going to be a better place to live?

September 7

Thoreau wrote, "Poverty . . . is life near the bone, where it is sweetest." It's possible to have too much in life. Too many clothes jade our appreciation for new ones; too much money can put us out of touch with life; too much free time can dull the edge of the soul. Benedict's lesson to us all is that we need sometimes to come very near the bone so that we can taste the marrow of life rather than its superfluities.

September 8

People want change but they want it to come without discomfort. They want to rock no boats, make no waves. They think that people can be talked into change, but the fact is that most people only change when they have no choice. Think of the great attitudinal changes in your life. What incidents happened that made change necessary? What kind of things are you yourself doing to bring necessary changes now? After all, one of the functions of leadership is to lead.

September 9

The world is filled with churchgoers and the world is filled with the obscenely poor. Go figure.

September 10

It all seems so futile, this reckless generosity of Benedict's. What good can one vial of oil possibly do? Edward Everett wrote, "I am only one but I am one. I cannot do everything, but I can do something; and though I cannot do everything, whatever I can do, I will do, so help me God." Maybe it isn't oil that Benedict wants us to give. Maybe it is hope.

September 11

St. Benedict, one man who built an entire lifestyle around a different set of values than were then in popular coinage and put an entire world on notice about them. Those values—community, hospitality, stewardship, humility, prayer, peace, justice—are as important to civilized life now as they were 1,500 years ago. That's why Agapitus went to the monastery for help. The question for us today is: Whose values prevailed in the end—Benedict's or the cellarer's? Why? What values do you model for other people? Do your values nourish the poor?

September 12

Joanna Macy wrote, "The heart that breaks open can contain the whole universe." The secret is that to be passionately compassionate the heart must "break" open, not simply be pried open or teased open or coaxed open. We must learn to feel what we see. The pragmatist reads about Benedict's extravagant generosity and accuses him of jeopardizing the life of his own community. The seer knows that Benedict was not doing "charity"; Benedict was doing love. Benedict's heart had broken and he could do no other. And you?

September 13

The problem in the world is not the availability of resources; the real problem in the world is the distribution of resources. The problem is not that we lack the technology to feed every woman, man, and child on earth; the problem is that we lack the political will. The *zaddik* taught, "If anyone comes to you asking for help, do not say in refusal, 'Trust in God and God will help you.' Rather, act as if there were no God, and no one there to help except you."

September 14

Diane Johnson writes, "We are surrounded by the enraged." These words have a prophetic ring to them. Every day the number of the inhumanly poor increases. Only love equally enraged can possibly restore the balance. What will you give of yourself, as Benedict did, to begin to reestablish it?

September 15

Benedict is painfully clear: when we become immersed in our own problems and plans and forget the plight of the poor, we do not deserve to exist. St. Basil, another monastic, taught, "The bread in your cupboard belongs to the hungry person; the coat hanging unused in your closet belongs to the one who needs it; the shoes rotting in your closet belong to the one who has no shoes; the money which you hoard away belongs to the poor." Don't miss the message: everything we own belongs to the poor who have as much right to what comes from the hand of God as we do but less education and opportunity to get it.

September 16

Trust is the counterpoint of generosity. I can only give my own possessions to someone who needs them more than I do if I truly believe that, by God's goodness, they will come back to me when I need them. Generosity is easy. It makes us look good. It's trust that's hard to come by. Somewhere there is a squirrel in each of us, hoarding, preserving, hiding against the unseen winters of life. Then it's time, perhaps, to remember Celia Layton

Thaxter's dictum: "Sad soul, take comfort, nor forget that sunrise never failed us yet."

September 17

The poor cellarer. I bet he worried all his life.

September 18

Robert Eliot wrote, "Rule #1 is, don't sweat the small stuff. Rule #2 is, it's all small stuff." There comes a point in life when we have to stop exaggerating our needs, our problems, and our importance. Benedict had arrived at that point; his cellarer had not.

September 19

The nice thing about Benedict is that he knew the value of public witness. So many times we do good as if it were evil, quietly, silently, so no one will see it, so we don't cause any stir. Not Benedict, he made a public act out of what was first meant to be a private beneficence but then became a matter of moral teaching. Have you ever taken part in a public demonstration? Why not? If you really believe in the issue, why are you dealing with it only in private?

September 20

The monks who saw Benedict throw the vial of oil out the window got the lesson of their lives in freedom. Name three things you own that you value very much. Now, in your mind's eye, throw each of them out the window one at a time. What happens to you when you do it? "You will become as small as your greatest desire; as great as your dominant aspiration," James Allen wrote. Are you free yet?

September 21

Today, give something you value away. It will enrich the life of another and it will liberate you, as well. The poor teach us how little we really need in life.

September 22

Did you do it? Did you give something away? Why not? Is security your trap too?

September 23

George Bernard Shaw wrote, "There are two tragedies in life. One is to lose your heart's desire. The other is to gain it." Have you suffered yet from getting what you wanted in life? You will. Then, the struggle becomes learning to live with what we created. The trick is to hold everything in life so lightly that only death can kill us.

September 24

One of the characters in Enid Bagnold's *National Velvet* says with simple wisdom, "She keeps 'er brains in 'er heart, and that's where they ought ter be." The monastery's cellarer had his brains where they should be—and failed the world. Benedict thought with his heart and gave life. Where are your brains—in your head or in your heart?

September 25

"I give you my naked soul / like a statue unveiled," Juana de Ibarbarou wrote. Would anyone know your naked soul if they saw it? Do you know it yourself? Is it the soul of the cellarer or the soul of Benedict? The poor and the oppressed are knocking at your door now. Who will answer this time?

September 26

Why was Benedict so angry? Because the monastery had been given a chance to be generous and failed the test? No, because the monastery had been given a chance to love dangerously and had opted to be safe instead. Have you ever loved dangerously? What happened to you as a result?

September 27

There is a very thin line between taking care of myself and being selfish. To discover the difference between them just ask yourself why you are doing what you are doing. And tell yourself the truth.

September 28

Good sense makes the world go round but risk is what changes it. "One person traveling opposite the flow," Noah ben Shea writes, "is more clearly noticed than all who travel together." For once in your life, go against the flow.

September 29

Learning to be angry about the right things in life is one of life's great virtues. It is a sign of great holiness, a memory of Jesus in the Temple of God on Mount Sinai. Have you developed it yet?

September 30

Every time you find yourself being too sensible, being a careful cellarer, take a deep breath and do something wild. Who knows? It could save the world—and it may even help you.

GOTH AND POOR MAN

A Call to Peace and Nonviolence

A Goth by the name of Zalla was beating and torturing a poor, local farmer because he wanted his money. The poor peasant, who was without any protection, did the only thing he could think of to save his life and get Zalla to go away. He told the Goth that he had no money to give him because he had given all his money to the local monastery. In those troubled days, however, that argument cut no ice at all. To an Arian Goth, monks were no more sacrosanct than anyone else. On the contrary. Zalla, infuriated, bound and tied the farmer's hands together, mounted his horse, and forced the man to lead him to the monk who had the money. No difference to him whom he terrorized.

And that's where the story takes a different turn. The Goth, seeing Benedict reading at the entrance of the monastery, screamed at him, "Get up! Do you hear? Get up and give back the money this man left with you!" But Benedict didn't move.

In fact, Benedict hardly looked at Zalla at all. Instead, he looked hard at the ropes on the frightened farmer's wrists. And when he looked at them, the ropes simply shriveled up and fell away. The farmer was free. Instantly.

And so in a way was Zalla. The Goth, completely undone, powerless in the face of such a powerful spirit, fell to his knees in front of Benedict. But Benedict, never rising from his place, had the monks take Zalla inside for food and drink and then sent him on his way with the instruction that he should not be so cruel again.

This story defies instinct, stops us cold, and teaches us plenty:

Strength of spirit is immovable.

Kindness and calm can disarm the wildest of rages.

Real kindness knows no limits.

October 1

In a world full of enemies, Benedict refused to be enemy to anyone. Whose enemy are you? Why? What do you gain by it? Don't you wonder what would happen if you simply invited them in for something to eat and drink? Aw, go ahead.

October 2

What's the use of returning rage for rage—besides equalizing the noise level in the room, of course? Try it. Name three things you think rage does. (Pause.) That's what I thought. Useless.

October 3

Kindness is a strange thing. In the end it is the only thing that prevails in our relationships—not intelligence, not power, not social status—just kindness. Think of one person who has been kind to you. Have you ever told them?

October 4

"Kindness," Joseph Joubert wrote, "is loving people more than they deserve." Admit it. You expected Benedict to forgive the Goth but you did not expect him to invite him in for lunch! I mean, enough is enough, right?

October 5

Imagine. Benedict just sat there reading while the enemy approached on horseback. After all, what could the Goth really do to hurt him? Take what he had? He didn't have anything worth fighting for. Take his life? That would go someday anyway. Give him orders? He had no intention of taking them. Now that's power. What are you so afraid of losing that gives everyone in the world power over you? Why?

October 6

There's nothing more devastating to the powerful than having some little person defy their orders. I wonder why, in a world where the orders of the powerful cause so much of the agony of the powerless, we don't do more of it. Do you know the reasons for that? What do you think of those motives?

October 7

"Most people prefer to be slaves," Thomas Jefferson wrote. Is that true? What's easier for you: doing what you're told to do whatever its effects on others, or questioning what you're told to do that doesn't seem to be right? Like learning to kill in the military, maybe, or barring women from positions in the church.

October 8

Joan Borysenko writes, "The question is not whether we will die, but how we will live." We can live kind or we can live tough. Choose. What difference would that choice have made this week?

October 9

"Each small task of everyday is part of the total harmony of the universe," St. Thérèse of Lisieux said. When Benedict concentrated on the ropes on the farmer's wrists instead of on the screaming demands of the Goth, the universe became a calmer, kinder place. What demands are now being made on you that you should ignore for the sake of the universe?

October 10

It is so easy to hate the oppressor, to make enemies of the people who run the systems that rest heavy on our backs—the politicians who create the national policies, the bankers who set interest rates, the corporation executives who decide the wage and benefit formulas, the men who personify a sexist church. But hate and confrontation are not the same thing. It is absolutely imperative to confront evil. It is also necessary to be both honest and kind. What a rare combination.

October 11

"Life is an adventure in forgiveness," Norman Cousins said. Either that or it is a tragedy in retaliation and rejection, revenge and hot resentment. Which of those climates are you living in right now?

October 12

Here's the crux of the story: strength is not what we are trained to think it is. Benedict is much stronger than Zalla. What strengths do you have? What strength should you have?

October 13

Zalla was a Christian heretic but Benedict refused to read him out of his life. He took him into the monastery and treated him like family, in fact. He told him to quit abusing people but he apparently said not one word about changing his beliefs. Who are we calling heretics these days? Are we doing nearly as well with them as a church as Benedict did? Who are the heretics in your family, your office, your club? How did you treat them the last time you met?

October 14

Who do you know right now whose wrists are tied in life? What can you do today to help free them?

October 15

There's a touch of Zalla the heretic, barbarian, and bully in each of us. Tell me, Zalla, before whom have you wilted in life? What power did you see in the other that disarmed your own? What did you learn about yourself in that situation?

October 16

"The strength of a person lies in finding out the way God is going and going that way," Harriet Beecher Stowe wrote. Where do you and God diverge in life? How do you account for this difference between the way you see life and the way God sees life? What are you doing about it?

October 17

Shakespeare wrote, "It is excellent to have a giant's strength but it is tyrannous to use it like a giant." What does that mean? What would strength be good for if you didn't use it like a giant? Who has the giant's strength in this story: Zalla or Benedict? Why?

October 18

"If you can keep your head when all about you are losing theirs . . ." you will be considered insane. But that's all right. What good is sanity if it's not strange?

October 19

Beaten to a pulp, the farmer is ready to do anything to get Zalla out of his life. So he lies. Now here's the question. Some people are beaten down by poverty and would do anything to get it out of their lives. So, are the people who lie about the unclaimed money they earn while on welfare to be condemned or not? Think about it.

October 20

Kindness is a strong and valiant virtue that we have turned into plastic and social grace. Kindness is what saves lives and gives love to the dead of spirit and the dark of heart. In that case, has anyone ever really been kind to you? Better yet, have you ever really been kind to anyone else? It's a more precious commodity than we think.

October 21

To unbind the wrists of the poor and oppressed means to do more than to pat them on the head and throw them crumbs. It means being willing to stand up to the powers that oppress them. So now, think again. When were you last kind?

October 22

It's the substance with which we nourish our own souls that makes us strong enough to free others. Benedict was sitting in the doorway of the monastery studying Scripture when Zalla

attacked him. It was hours of holy reading that made him fear-
less of Zalla, not a list of religious rules, good as they may have
been. What's more important to you: the reading or the rules?

October 23

Here's the tough one: if Zalla hadn't tormented the farmer and
the farmer hadn't lied, and Zalla hadn't forced the peasant to
take him to Benedict, would Zalla ever have come to recognize
holiness? "Sin is behovable," the mystic Julian of Norwich says.
We have a lot to learn from sin, in other words. What kindness
have you learned from yours?

October 24

"I am cruel only to be kind," Shakespeare's character Iago de-
clares. It's a good lesson. Instead of telling a person our truth, we
choose instead to be "kind," to listen as if we agree. As a result,
we mislead them into loving us, or hating someone else, or living
in ways we know are wrong for them. Don't ever rationalize it;
that's kindness gone awry. "Say yes when you mean yes and no
when you mean no," Scripture teaches. And Scripture knows.

October 25

Benedict does not temporize with cruelty. He doesn't reason
with it or try to cajole it. He simply undoes its effects. That's
kindness. To both parties.

October 26

Thoreau wrote, "Most of us lead lives of quiet desperation."
Even Zalla. So be kind.

October 27

"The dew of compassion is a tear," Lord Byron wrote. Have
you ever cried for someone else's pain? Be honest. What is that
saying about you?

October 28

There is no one impervious to kindness and conversion. "The
Buddha exists in the robber and the dice player; the robber exists in the Brahmin," Hermann Hesse wrote. Benedict and Zalla
know it's true.

October 29

Listen to someone today. Don't set them up. Don't ask the
proper question and then interrupt them when they start to
answer. Listen. That in itself is an act of kindness.

October 30

Don't be fooled by all the pap. It's not easy to be kind. It costs.
Are you up to it? Like Benedict, it will interrupt what you are

doing and it will leave you with all the Zallas and all the peasants of the world on your doorstep. Don't leap. Think about it.

October 31

Today is the eve of All Saints Day. Robert Louis Stevenson wrote, "The saints are sinners who keep on trying." Good. I still have time.

CHILD RAISED FROM THE DEAD

A Call to Justice and Compassion

If there is anything to remember about Benedict of Nursia, it is that he did not purport to be a wonder worker. He did not stump miracles. So, the setting of this story is an interesting one. One day Benedict was working in the fields when one of the local farmers came running to the monastery carrying the dead body of his only son. Beside himself with grief, the father begged Benedict to bring his son back to life. Benedict was reluctant even to try. "Stand back, Brothers," he said to the monastics there. "Only the Holy Fathers, the Apostles, raise from the dead." The message was a clear one: our work is to be mindful, perhaps, but our work is not to be miracle workers.

And then Benedict asked the question that gives us pause. "Why," he said to the distraught farmer, "are you trying to avoid what falls to us all?" Death, he implied starkly, is a part of life.

But the farmer would not relent. This boy was his past and his future, the center of his world. Enraged, he swore at Benedict and refused to leave until Benedict did what he could to reverse his life's tragedy.

And Benedict understood. He threw himself down beside the boy, prayed his heart out, and the boy stirred to life again.

It is a story of human suffering and human response that is repeated every day of our lives. The implications are clear:

Every day the suffering of the world look to the secure of the world to do something to save them from even more disaster.

No one has a right to preach platitudes to the poor. We must each do something in their regard.

It is not our job to work miracles but it is our task to try.

Death is indeed a necessary part of life but everything that looks dead is not and, in fact, may really be the beginning of new life in us.

November 1

Today the Christian world remembers those who have gone through life and all its trials but triumphed in the end. The saints, we call them. To lose them leaves a gap in the human community. This whole event is very bad, we tell ourselves, but down deep we never really forget that their presence in life made life better for us all. It is that truth to which Benedict called the farmer. All death is welcome. No death is really the end because what that person did lives on in us. It is that awareness to which, in the course of our own small deaths, we all must cling, however much we resist them. All life, our lives too, is meant to make a difference for many.

November 2

Today is the day we realize that loss, however holy, is still loss. Today we understand the farmer's impatience with the current of life. All of us, at one time or another, want things to change faster than they do. It is All Souls Day, that unknown amount of time between death and resurrection to new life that reminds us that waiting is part of the process of finally coming to wholeness.

November 3

Death, Benedict shows the farmer and his community, is an invitation to new life. Mary Magdalen, for instance, after the death of Jesus, rose again, this time with courage and purpose. The little people for whom Jesus' whole ministry had been spent rose again, this time with new conviction and certainty. Rising again is the central message of the Christian tradition. What in you needs to rise again after your own losses? What resurrection miracle should you, like Benedict, be for someone else right now?

November 4

The Russian writer Dostoyevsky wrote, "To live without hope is to cease to live." When the farmer rushes to the monastery to give Benedict the body of his dead son, hope goes on a rampage. The world comes alive with possibility. What could be becomes more real than what is. Realists dampen hope in the name of good sense, of course. But what really makes more sense: to be smothered by the unbearable or to live with one eye on what might be if we just all tried a little harder?

November 5

When the damp of death is upon our hearts, it is very difficult to believe that life can come out of it. That is why the farmer and his dead son are as important to Benedict as Benedict is to them. Benedict may never have come to know the amount of life in himself if the farmer had not demanded he exert it. In what way is new life being demanded from you right now? Are you willing to move beyond what is already dead in your life to claim it?

November 6

In 1909 Admiral Perry discovered the North Pole, a bleak and barren wasteland. Surely some people questioned the value of the find. Yet, the North Pole may be the richest center of natural resources on earth. So often what we strive for looks lifeless when we get it. But, who knows? There may well be life under the cold crust of it after all.

November 7

Benedict's response to the poor farmer, "Why are you seeking to avoid what is part of every life?" comes very close to being an "offer it up" speech. But the farmer won't do it. The farmer is smart enough to realize that God does not will our distress. Circumstances cause it and circumstances can change it. Benedict learns that we are all to be a part of the liberation movement in life, not silent bystanders in a world oppressive of far too many people.

November 8

Issa wrote on the death of his child, "Dew evaporates and all our world is dew . . . so dear, so refreshing, so fleeting." Death is about learning to let go in life, yes, but it is also about clinging better to love while we can. What do you love that you are not loving enough right now?

November 9

The Rabbi of Brastlav taught, "If you won't be better tomorrow than you were today, then what do you need tomorrow for?" There is a lesson in today for us all. What is it? How will you be better tomorrow because of it?

November 10

It is the persistence of the farmer in his outlandish request and the reluctance of Benedict to give in to it that gives us the best insight into ourselves, perhaps. The demands of the poor irritate us because of welfare fraud, because of our own desires to accumulate, because of our commitment to the truisms of rugged individualism. But those things are not ours to judge. What we forget is that God will judge the poor on honesty. The rest of us God will judge on generosity. Now which one of us is holiest?

November 11

When Benedict realized that the farmer was demanding that he perform a miracle over the body of his dead son, it must have been a terrible moment for that honest man. Resurrections were, he knew, beyond him. We know the feeling. So much is beyond us too: family problems, professional challenges, world events.

But, like Benedict, we are not excused from the responsibility to respond to them. The effort is up to us; the results are up to God.

November 12

John Greenleaf Whittier puts every spring of life into unusual focus. He wrote, "The dark night is over and dawn has begun: Rise, hope of the ages, arise like the sun, All speech, flow to music, all hearts, beat as one!" Spring is our chance to try again to make the world right. What one thing can you do today to make your own life right again?

November 13

Benedict and his monks were working their fields when the farmer arrived, desperate and looking for miracles. The monastics were their steady, predictable selves. The only thing is that, like us, they forgot that life is not about being steady. Life is about being involved in the right things at the right time. Here it was a matter of life and death. If you are not giving attention to any of the life-and-death matters of this time, the question is not, Are you a good person? The question is, Are you really a spiritual one?

November 14

Antoine de Saint-Exupéry wrote, "A single event can awaken within us a stranger totally unknown to us. To live is to be slowly born." That's what happened to Benedict. Something new came to life in him because of his contact with the boy. What have you discovered about yourself recently that you never knew before?

November 15

It is the anger of the farmer that shocks us. He swore at Benedict. This is not a polite request, in other words; this is a demand that we are dealing with. The poor, you see, have the right to prevail upon us all. We owe them the fruits of the earth that were meant for them but taken away by an industrial system that rewards those who bear least its daily burdens. We must remember that charity is not enough; it is justice that is required.

November 16

"Growth is the only evidence of life," John Henry Newman wrote. The farmer's son was dead but Benedict and his monastics needed to grow into a new understanding of life, as well. They were far too content with what they were doing to realize that they needed to be open to something else. A simple farmer called them all out of their routine. None of us like to have our well-ordered lives interrupted, but interruptions are precisely what jolt us into new consciousness. What interruption of your routine is making new demands on you?

November 17

Benedict was making a point to the farmer that all of us need to learn at some time or other. There are things in every life that need to die. The function of the past is to bring us to the present, not to obstruct it. What is dying in your life right now? Let it go.

November 18

Sometimes growth comes where we least expect it. The farmer did not expect that it would be death that would increase his faith; Benedict did not expect that it would be someone outside the monastery who would call him to grow in trust. It is those moments in life that unmask us in which we grow the most. Has it happened to you yet?

November 19

In the United States alone thirty-seven million people use food pantries and soup kitchens, while the rest of the country smothers in affluence. The poor carry their dying to the doors of the secure everyday. We are being asked to work miracles on their behalf, and, like Benedict, we say we are not able. And yet, just like in Benedict's time, God may simply be waiting for us to try.

November 20

"It's too bad that dying is the last thing we do because it could teach us so much about life," Robert Herford said. We're always on our way to what's next. Imagine how happy life would be if we could just allow ourselves to enjoy the moment we're in, to learn from it, to taste and savor and lick its depth.

November 21

Today is the feast of St. Anselm of Canterbury, the Benedictine abbot, theologian, and philosopher of the twelfth century who was called the "Father of Scholasticism" because of his ordering of theological thought in a period when schooling was rare, books were hand-lettered, and communication was nonexistent. Here was a man, in other words, who did what had to be done against all odds. As you and I must do now. What is it that you think you cannot do, but must do? Don't even flinch. It's been done before you.

November 22

Ralph Waldo Emerson wrote, "God enters by a private door into every individual." For Benedict it was the surprise visit of the farmer, the reality of the dead son. What is the door that opened God for you? What door is opening for you now that you are resisting?

November 23

The important thing about this miracle of Benedict is that he didn't think he could do it and he didn't think that he couldn't do it. Miracles, you see, are out of our hands. Name a miracle that you performed in life when you thought that it was least possible.

November 24

Everybody wants to grow but nobody wants to die to do it. The problem is, as any spring seed knows, that's the only way.

November 25

A Chinese proverb teaches, "People in the West are always getting ready to live." Imagine the waste of wishing, planning, saving your life away. What are you getting ready for that needs to be done now? Remember: there are some things in life that are worth doing poorly.

November 26

The poet Edna St. Vincent Millay wrote, "My candle burns at both ends; it will not last the night; but ah, my foes, and oh, my friends—it gives a lovely light." The point of life is not to succeed. The point of life is to die trying.

November 27

The philosopher Heraclitus taught, "You can't step into the same river twice." In other words, life is always changing. The most stable of relationships change character as they go. Life is simply one long series of changes, a collection of small deaths. The lesson is to learn from one so that we can live better in the next.

November 28

The monastics who watched Benedict give himself entirely to the cause of the dead boy and the frantic father learned a great lesson. They learned that it is one thing to work in the fields and say we are about life and growing things. It is entirely another to recognize death when we see it and change our own lives to bring life about. What should you be about that you say you do not have the time or talent to attend to now? Who will not live because you have denied your time to them?

November 29

Oscar Wilde wrote, "For those who live more lives than one, more deaths than one must die." It is a painful, wonderful thought. We will go through life dying a thousand deaths. The children shall leave home; the house will be sold; the jobs will change; the character of faith shall ebb and deepen. But after each one of them, new life will come. The boy Benedict raised from the dead was not the boy who died and neither are we after many deaths, many resurrections.

November 30

"One day a group of people will go to a cemetery," John McLelland wrote in *The Crown and the Crocodile*, "hold a brief service, and return home. All except one; that one will be you." Ah, yes. And then, if all these other days have been well-lived, a new kind of life will begin.

WORLD IN A RAY OF LIGHT
A Call to Contemplative Vision

Of all the stories told about Benedict, this one may be the most impacting of all on our own lives. Most of us will never work miracles or found monasteries or humble invaders, that's for sure. But one thing we can all learn to do is to see. This story is about a special kind of seeing.

Benedict left the company of a neighboring abbot after an evening's conversation about the spiritual life. The period predates both universities and books, remember, let alone televisions and computers. Personal conversation was the key to learning then—a factor that may well explain the popularity of gurus and spiritual masters in that culture. At any rate, people came in droves to talk to Benedict about their spiritual questions, the great no less than the simple.

On this particular night, it is the Abbot Severanus, a deeply prayerful person himself, with whom Benedict has been talking. But then, retiring to his own room, alone and filled with ideas on the spiritual life, Benedict suddenly began to see what he had never seen before: the sky filled with light "more brilliant than the sun, and with it every trace of darkness cleared away." Then, according to the Dialogues, Benedict "saw the whole world as in a single ray of light." More than that, while he watched, Benedict saw the soul of his friend Abbot Germanus taken into heaven. Astounded by the sight and intent on testing his own perceptions, Benedict called on Abbot Severanus, a solid and dependable person, to look at the sky and sent a monk to inquire about Germanus as well. The confirmation was clear: Severanus too saw the vision and Germanus, he learned, had indeed died at the very time. Benedict had developed sight and insight. Benedict had begun to see things differently.

The implications for us and our own lives abound:

The spiritual life enlarges a person's vision.

When we begin to see as God sees, we see far beyond ourselves.

Contemplation is a very human thing; all of us are called to be contemplatives.

December 1

On this day in 1955, Rosa Parks defied the Montgomery, Alabama, busing laws and refused to yield her seat to a white man. She was a visionary. She saw a world where blacks and whites would both be treated as human beings and began the movement by demanding it for herself. What new way of living do you see in your vision of the world? What one thing will you do today to hasten the coming of that vision?

December 2

"Vision," Jonathan Swift wrote, "is the art of seeing things invisible." Every one of us carries a personal vision in our own heart. What is yours and how does it differ from life as you know it now?

December 3

On this day in 1967, Dr. Christian Barnard performed the first human heart transplant operation in Cape Town, South Africa. He was criticized for being premature with the process, but, after him, organ transplants became commonplace. What is it that you know should be done but think is too soon to do? Are you being wise or simply safe?

December 4

What Benedict saw outside of himself is what he already had inside of himself—breadth of soul, compassion, and openheartedness. What is inside of you right now? Think.

December 5

Here's the real beauty of the story: Severanus saw the vision too. It wasn't a spiritual trick of Benedict's; it was the natural by-product of the spiritual life. It's what we take into a thing that we get out of it, in other words. What are you carrying inside of you right now? Hope? Cynicism? Self-centeredness? Open-mindedness? What? Most of all, what is it doing to you?

December 6

A Hindustani proverb teaches, "No proof is required of what is before our eyes." Think of your own last twenty-four hours. Now think of your next twenty-four hours. What is before your eyes? What is it saying to you spiritually? What does it demand of you?

December 7

Remember that it was after they had been discussing spiritual things that Benedict's vision was enlarged to include the whole world. It takes a spiritual sensitivity to hold the whole globe and all its needs in our heart. Any spirituality that makes our hearts narrower than the globe is a bogus spirituality for sure.

December 8

"Wonder is the beginning of wisdom," a Greek proverb reminds us. Maybe, but we are more prone to evaluate anything that is different from us instead of standing in awe of it. Imagine what could happen in the world if we stood in awe of African culture, in awe of strong women and gentle men, in awe of new ideas and new questions. Instead, we block them or reject them or fear them. Then we miss our chance to appreciate the whole world.

December 9

When Benedict and Severanus talked together they both grew in soul and insight. To whom do you talk about ideas? Who stretches your soul?

December 10

Everybody has to learn from somebody. Benedict respected Severanus as much as Severanus respected him. The relationship deepened both of them. Who is your teacher and who may be learning from you?

December 11

Never think you've arrived. There's always something else to
learn in life. What new work are you beginning right now? In
what way is it enlarging your vision, enriching your soul? If it
isn't, start something that will.

December 12

A recent study indicates that the brains of nuns who stayed intellectually active far into their nineties showed much less atrophy
at the time of autopsy than the brains of their contemporaries who
had long before "retired." The conclusion seems to be that if you
want to live well while you live long, it is imperative to live life
fully, to go on envisioning the world. Old age is a lie. Don't quit.

December 13

"Contemplation" and "cloister" are not synonyms. Cloister
is simply one of many vehicles to contemplation. Some people
need to be cloistered to see God in life; others see God in the
faces of the poor. Otherwise, the Jesus who walked the roads of
Galilee curing and teaching crowds doesn't qualify. And that's a
silly thought, isn't it?

December 14

We talk about contemplation as if it were some kind of spiritual magic. Actually, the contemplative is the person who is so
immersed in the will of God that they come to see the world

as God sees the world. The fact is that all of us are called to be contemplatives.

December 15

If we don't begin soon to realize that we are all citizens of the world, if we don't begin to see the entire globe as our home instead of simply the country or city or neighborhood in which we now live, we may soon lose it all. If Benedict is teaching us anything in this story, it is surely the fact that nothing less than the entire world must be our concern.

December 16

Tomorrow, in anticipation of Christmas, the monastic community begins to review its vision of Jesus by chanting ancient prayers known now as the "O Antiphons." Each of these chants recalls a different aspect of the Christ-life to which we are called. Write your own "O Antiphons" by naming seven qualities of Jesus which you believe should be an important part of your own vision of life.

December 17

"O Wisdom," the community prays today in its anticipation of new grace in life. It's important to realize that wisdom and education are not the same thing. Education provides the experiences we need in order to manage our lives. Wisdom, on the other hand, is what we learn as a result of the experiences we have.

December 18

"O Adonai," the community sings today. "O God of All," we chant. When we build a vision of life it is necessary to realize that Jesus must be the center of it—not our institutions, good as they may be; not our plans or personal talents, necessary as they are.

December 19

"O Root of Jesse," the community remembers today. It takes generations to build the Christ-vision in the world, just as it took generations after Jesse to prepare for the coming of the Christ. It is our task to root ideas now that will bring the next generation to wholeness.

December 20

"O Key of David," we say at Vespers today. We're all looking for the keys to life—the key to success, the key to happiness, the key to serenity. And we're always looking for it somewhere other than in the life and teachings of Jesus. The problem is that we already have it and don't recognize it. What key in your present life are you avoiding, resisting, overlooking, rejecting?

December 21

"O Radiant Dawn," we chant today. We look for light everywhere. But it was night when Benedict saw the vision of his life. That's what usually happens to us too. Just when we think that light will never come into our lives again, we begin to see a whole new world around us.

December 22

"O God of All the Earth," we pray today. We get a chance today to realize that we are not the beginning and the end of the universe. We are part of a vision of humankind, seen in Jesus but yet to be achieved in us—a vision of global sharing, universal peace, and individual security. If we all want it so much, what is delaying its coming? I'm serious. What is it?

December 23

"O Emmanuel," we sing tonight, not so much in hope as in recognition. After all, Jesus—Emmanuel, God with us—has already come. It is not a matter now of Christ's being where we are; it is a matter of our being conscious of where Christ is in life. And where he is not as well. Where is Christ for you this Christmas? And is there a place in your life that you know down deep is not in the spirit of Christ at all?

December 24

Christmas Eve. Not only did the angels recognize the vision of Jesus but they announced it to all the rest of it. There's the test. It's so easy to make the Christ-life a private, personal, comfortable thing. As if that's what the Christ who cured lepers, broke the

Sabbath on behalf of the poor, and contested with the establishment came to teach. What could possibly diminish the vision more than that attitude toward religion?

December 25

Jesus is the vision of what we can each be, are meant to be, must be. Christmas is not a fairy tale; Christmas is a gift of new life; Christmas is a mandate to be more than we have been before. Christmas is the vision of the Vision.

December 26

At first it seems to be a contradiction: at the very time that Benedict saw the whole world in one glance, he saw only one person in it. But once we begin to look at the world as God looks at the world, that's exactly what happens. We see every person in it as unique, precious, all-absorbing. People cease to be numbers and stereotypes and races and sexes. They become individuals to us. Every one of them on their twisted, limping way to God.

December 27

Benedict had a powerful personal vision but he also had it confirmed. Point: no matter how certain our insights, it's important to let other people consider them with us. Not to change them or obstruct them, necessarily, but certainly to test their quality, their value, their meaning for the world as well as for ourselves.

December 28

The Scripture says, "Without vision, the people perish." Every life, in other words, should have a purpose. What's yours? Be careful. If it's not big enough, you will live a very stunted existence in a very small world that dulls early and goes too drab too soon. What are you reaching for that is worth the measure of a life?

December 29

Name ten things you know about any other ten countries on earth. Stretch your vision.

December 30

The great visionaries of the world—people like the scientist, the philanthropist, the doctor—all set out to make life better for all of us. Name three things that you have done to improve the life of strangers around you. That's OK, don't get discouraged. That's what the Christmas season is all about: starting over to bring Christ into the world.

December 31

When we fail "to see the whole world in one ray of light," we imprison ourselves inside our own small selves without ideas, without experiences, without love. Make this next year a fuller one. Your soul will burst from the beauty and bigness of it.